AMERICA'S
HISTORIC
TRAILS

AMERICA'S HISTORIC TRAILS

JOHN THOMPSON

NATIONAL GEOGRAPHIC

WASHINGTON, D.C.

NATIONAL HISTORIC TRAILS

◆ ◆ ◆

INTRODUCTION

They etch our landscape like lines written in fading ink left for future generations to discover. Some run east to west, others north to south, following the dictates of geography, war, and weather. Ranging in length from 54 to more than 2,000 miles, they proceed by fits and starts, have variations and branches. And each one tells a story—goals, obstacles, turning points, and climaxes are all there, as are heroes and villains, happy endings and sad. Our national historic trails are gripping stories of people on the move, each story a crucial chapter in American history.

What makes for a national historic trail? First of all, it has to be historically significant, particularly as a major route of migration, trade, exploration, communication, or military action. Then, the trail must have "potential for public recreational use or historical

interest." Any individual or organization can propose a trail for national historic status, but only Congress can designate one. In 1968, Congress passed the National Trails System Act; ten years later the first national historic trails—the Oregon, Mormon Pioneer, Iditarod, and Lewis and Clark—were added to the system.

There are currently 8 scenic and 14 historic trails. Unlike the scenic, the historic trails are generally not continuous. The historic trails cross private as well as public land; in places they fork into multiple routes or disappear from the historic record altogether. They may go through shopping centers, military installations, Indian reservations, as well as some of the most breathtaking scenery in the country. You can drive sections of the original trails—after all, some of them were started as transportation

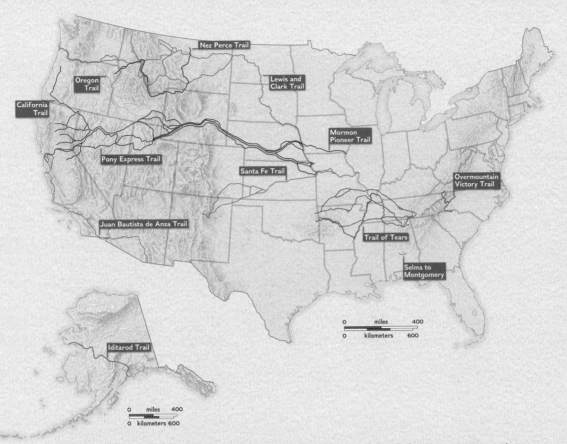

Historic trails reflect the triumphs of the American spirit as well as some of its darker moments. Some emigrants journeyed with dreams of a better life, while the Nez Perce and the Cherokee fled their homes with broken hearts.

routes. You can also hike or paddle, or even go by covered wagon or horseback, through miles of unchanged terrain. The point is that these trails are often abstract ideas as much as real, usable trails. The difference between their original and current look reflects the changes wrought by a growing nation. Take the famous Oregon Trail, for example. Hundreds of thousands of emigrants traveled this east-west corridor, and you can still find hundreds of miles of wagon-wheel ruts. But people also settled along the way. The trail's purpose was to convey people from one place to another; that done, the trail began bit by bit to disappear.

How, then, does one follow a trail that in a sense no longer exists? There are two basic approaches. One is to hit key sites along it—visiting, say, a fort, a state park, and a couple of museums, with time out for a hiking or biking trail. Thousands of travelers do this every year, though not necessarily traveling intentionally on a historic theme. Serious trail buffs take a different approach. They study maps, books, and journals, comparing the old trails to what's out there now. Then they take off for a week or two, or longer, and become trail sleuths—bumping along in four-wheel drives, scrambling through overgrown fields, looking for dips in the land or rust on a rock, any clue they can find. Many of these people belong to such organizations as the Oregon-California Trail Association and the

Overmountain Victory Trail Association—volunteer groups whose efforts have helped establish and preserve many of the trails.

However you do these trails, a magical thing happens. The modern world begins to grow fuzzy around the edges, and the past begins taking solid shape. When the destination becomes the trip itself, when the detours are more important than the straight line, the landscape acquires the deeply satisfying dimension of time, measured in centuries instead of minutes.

A growing number of historical markers and visitor centers along the way help piece things together. The National Park Service administers all but two of the historic trails—the Iditarod (Bureau of Land Management) and the Nez Perce Trail (U.S. Forest Service). And the dedicated efforts of local volunteer groups can never be overstated.

This book devotes a chapter to each of the 12 historic trails that have been at least partly developed for visitor use. Two new trails, designated in 2000, are still in the planning stages. One of them, El Camino Real de Tierra Adentro, or the Royal Road of the Interior, was a major trade route from San Juan Pueblo (north of Santa Fe, New Mexico) to El Paso, Texas, during the 17th to 19th centuries. Since the trail extended all the way to Mexico City, it could eventually become an international trail. Its designation as a historic corridor also adds texture to the story of the Santa Fe Trail, which continues northeast from El Camino Real. The 404-mile trail will likely include an auto tour route and several hiking segments. The other new trail, the Ala Kahakai, or the Trail by the Sea, is a 175-mile portion of an ancient route that circled the island of Hawaii. Starting at the island's north tip, the trail runs down the western coast and around to Hawaii Volcanoes National Park, passing lava fields, lagoons, valleys, and awe-inspiring cliffs. A highway already rims the Big Island, so the Ala Kahakai is a way of recognizing a historic route that predates Euro-American culture by hundreds of years.

The trails in the book appear with one story flowing into another, starting with the 1775 Juan Bautista de Anza Trail and ending with the 1965 Selma to Montgomery Trail. In each essay, we attempt to give an overall sense of the trail—its history, route, main landmarks, and present-day appearance.

One consistent theme that emerges is the courage it took the first pioneers to traverse them. No person could have completed any of these trails without a firmness of purpose in the face of great difficulties. Following any of the historic trails, we cannot help but wonder how we would have fared, and how we measure up on our own journeys through life.

We take these trails to learn the stories of our ancestors and to add to our own. Stories of fertile fields, gold in a stream, chance-of-a-lifetime adventure got our ancestors up and moving. We, too, start with a journey of the imagination. ◆

An adventurous and well-equipped backpacker hikes California's Anza-Borrego Desert State Park.

CHAPTER 1

JUAN BAUTISTA DE ANZA TRAIL

Proudly constructed out of sandstone rather than the more common adobe,
Mission San Carlos Borromeo del Rio Carmelo has welcomed visitors since the 18th century.

By order of the most excellent...Viceroy, Governor, and Captain-General of New Spain...for the establishment of the port of San Francisco....

—ANZA DIARY, 1775

San Francisco was nothing more than a dream when a scouting party led by Juan Bautista de Anza arrived in March 1776 and beheld the magnificent natural harbor now punctuated by the Golden Gate Bridge. Anza planted a cross to serve as a guide for ships and declared the area "a marvel of nature." The expedition chaplain, Pedro Font, imagined that if it could be settled like Europe "there would not be anything more beautiful in all the world." Anza's journey, which began five months and 1,200 miles earlier, had reached its goal; before the year was out, a presidio and a mission were built, giving Spain the foothold it wanted in Alta California. The oldest national historic trail and the only one to

traverse the desert Southwest, the Anza Trail grew from Spain's desire to keep the British and Russians off the Pacific Coast. The best way for Spain to establish a presence there was to blaze an overland trail from the Sonora region, in present-day Mexico, to present-day California. Such a trail would funnel emigrants, livestock, and military forces to the coast. But it followed a route strewn with hazards, which ranged from hostile Indians and dangerous river crossings to searing deserts and blinding dust storms.

Into this scenario steps 37-year-old Juan Bautista de Anza, a third-generation western-frontier soldier and desert-toughened Indian fighter. In 1774 he was captain of the Tubac Presidio, or fort, just north of

With the moon hovering above, the sunrise casts dramatic light on the spectacular, but forbidding, Borrego Badlands of southern California.

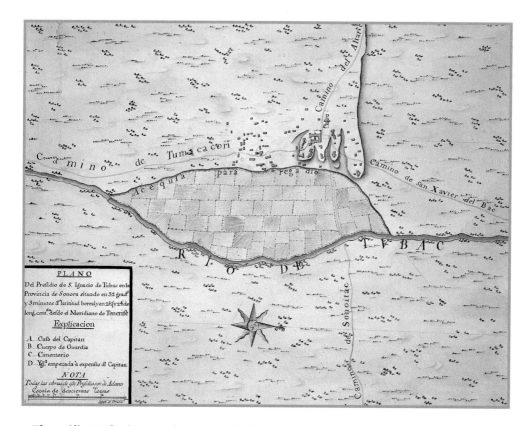

The presidio at Tubac in present-day Arizona is barely visible above the patchwork of fields shown in this 1767 drawing. The garrison's second commander, Juan Bautista de Anza, blazed the trail from Mexico to San Francisco.

the current border of Arizona and Mexico. To prove that an emigrant route was possible—and gain a little glory for himself—Anza financed an exploratory expedition across the desert to Monterey, noting watering holes and forage areas and making contact with natives. Anza largely followed old Indian trails and the footsteps of earlier Spaniards, some of whom predated him by 170 years. But he was the first to string all these trails together and make one continuous route to the future San Francisco. His real challenge lay not so much in charting a route but in what he did the following year—and what the current trail commemorates.

In October 1775 Anza took off from Tubac with 240 emigrants to found and colonize San Francisco. His sprawling caravan included 85 soldiers, cowboys, and muleteers; 155 women and children; 165 pack mules; 302 cattle; and 340 horses. He would have had 500 more horses, but a few weeks before departure, Apaches had stolen them. The first night out, a woman died during childbirth. Remarkably, it would be the only death on the entire 1,200-mile-long expedition. Her baby lived, as did two others born on the trail. Five long months later, the motley group arrived at the Royal Presidio of Monterey, from which Anza led a small reconnaissance party up to San Francisco Bay to pick a site for the new presidio. The expedition's success extended New Spain's influence far into California.

Along rivers and seashores, across deserts and mountains, the modern-day Anza Trail runs through a stunning variety of ecosystems on its way from Nogales, Arizona, to San Francisco. Though it generally cuts through private land—including numerous Indian reservations—you can trace most of the route on paved roadways. There are more than 60 historic sites associated with the trail, among them several beautifully restored missions as well as sections of the actual trail that can be traveled on foot, bike, or horseback. Communities and organizations are currently working to add another 600 miles to the official trail—a southern segment that would run from Nogales to Culiacan, Mexico—to recognize the beginnings of Anza's recruiting efforts and to create the world's first international historic trail.

Today, travelers have good reason for following this trail backwards. For one thing, it was established as a supply route, not a one-way road; Anza himself went up and down it twice. Also, tracking it back to its origins enables you to depart the heavily urbanized areas of California for some of the state's

The brilliant scarlet flowers of the ocotillo plant bring a burst of color to the southwestern desert. The branches of this woody shrub can reach 20 feet tall.

wilder corners—rather like taking a trip back in time. San Francisco's presidio still exists today, but only in name; there is little evidence of the Spanish colonial days. Still, the views of the bay and ocean from the presidio's lush hills remain. The presidio's 1,480 acres now sit within Golden Gate National Recreation Area, which offers about 100 miles of hiking and biking trails.

To explore an area little changed since Anza's time, you have to drive a couple of hours southeast of the city. Spreading over the shaggy brown hills of the Diablo Range, Henry W. Coe State Park preserves nearly 86,000 acres of grasslands, chaparral, and riparian woodland. The approach follows a slow, hairpin-turn, ten-mile road to the northwest corner of the park. For Anza it was a bit different. After planting his cross at the mouth of the bay, he and his scouting team dutifully surveyed the bay's eastern coast, then circled back through the hills before heading back to Monterey, where the bulk of his party waited. On their way through the hills in April, they named Coyote Creek and followed it down its East Fork, through the length of what is now Coe State Park. Anza is the first European known to have

The Pacific surf pounds the rock-strewn Gaviota Coast northwest of Santa Barbara. Spaniards named the rugged coastline

for the seagulls, or gaviotas, that patrolled the waters, which are a rich feeding ground for dolphins, seals, and whales.

traversed this area, though possibly others preceded him.

From the Coe visitor center, it's about a five-mile walk out to a refreshing swimming hole just below the confluence of the middle and eastern forks of Coyote Creek. In the dry summer season you can walk up the Narrows, the claustrophobic canyon that Anza negotiated with mules. As in his day, poison oak, ticks, and rattlesnakes still pose hazards. Grizzlies have vanished from the area, though a few mountain lions still roam.

Since Anza's time, countless visitors have enjoyed Monterey peninsula. The fog-wreathed headlands, cliffs, cypress stands, and coves of barking sea lions paint a compelling picture—so compelling that the area has been heavily developed. World-class golf courses, five-million-dollar homes, ritzy shops, and resorts all are part of the modern Monterey mosaic. Far fewer people have seen the place where the Anza party stayed before arriving in Monterey.

Situated just east of Santa Lucia Range, San Antonio de Padua was one of nine missions founded by Father Junipero Serra who lived from 1713-1784. The Mexican government began selling off the missions

Winds create wavelike patterns in California's Oceano Dunes. A rich but fragile ecosystem, the dunes harbor rare plants like the surf thistle.

in 1834, and they began to deteriorate, helped by earthquakes and other natural elements. But San Antonio and the other 20 missions connected by an early road system known as old Camino Real, have since been restored. San Antonio is particularly appealing because of its relative isolation, lying some 30 miles off U.S. 101. What you see now is pretty much what Anza would have seen— thick adobe walls, a lovely courtyard garden, a long cloister roofed in red tile, and a high-ceilinged, wood-beamed church. The walls and campanile are original. Fields of poppies and lupines skirt the property, which rolls unencumbered to the hills. "The site is very good," expedition chaplain Font wrote, "with fine lands, and plentiful water from the river which runs through this valley." He was less impressed with the local Indians: "They are small in body, degenerate, and ugly," their language consisting of "barbarous and ridiculous crackling and whistling and guttural sounds." Font was a good navigator and diarist, but also something of a prude. Anza was not particularly fond of him.

Publishing baron William Randolph Hearst owned much of the land you can see

Parched after having trekked though the desert, a Spanish soldier sips water offered by an Indian. This painting recreates the scene at the garrison of Tubac in 1774 when a pack train arrived from the south with supplies.

here. In 1940 he sold it to the U.S. Army, and it was thus preserved intact. From most directions, the view is of the natural world; to the south lie the Hearst ranch and some military buildings of Fort Hunter Liggett. Now, however, the U.S Navy plans to put a bombing range on the fort and to fly as many as 12 practice sorties a day; the Navy says noise pollution will be minimal, but opponents are dubious.

South about an hour and a half by car lies San Luis Obispo—a three-day journey for Anza. Those who miss San Antonio should at least see this mission, where Anza's party spent two nights in early March. Now an attractive college town near the coast, San Luis Obispo hums with youthful

energy. It's hard to get a feel for the trail here in the midst of a busy town, but the mission, a working parish, is an oasis of quiet dominated by a bronze statue of Father Serra, a sweet-smelling garden, and a museum of religious art, vestments, and Indian relics.

Positioned just north of the Mexican border, the 600,000-acre Anza-Borrego Desert State Park ranks as the largest state park in the contiguous 48 states. In late December 1775, a freak snowstorm trapped the Anza party for four days on the eastern edge of the park. As snow turned to rain they struggled through the Borrego Badlands, the cold rain dripping off the soldiers' broad-brimmed hats and ponytails and pooling in their blue serapes. Some 50 cattle

The Golden Gate Bridge majestically links San Francisco Bay and Marin County. In 1776 Juan Bautista de Anza's expedition

founded the Presidio de San Francisco not far from here, establishing the northernmost Spanish outpost in the New World.

wandered off and died in nearby quagmires. In Coyote Canyon the group celebrated Christmas Eve with a keg of brandy—and earned a scolding from Font, who only a few days earlier had taken the group to task for dancing a fandango.

Today the Borrego Badlands and Coyote Canyon are separated by the little town of Borrego Springs, which sits in the middle of the park. They remain rugged areas of hills and washes, easy to get lost in, although the quicksand that trapped Anza's cattle is no longer a problem. "The water table has dropped," explains interpretive specialist Joanie Cahill, "but the flip side is that there aren't as many springs. The temperature can reach 124°F in summer. A lot of people get dehydrated." In fact, regulations prohibit visitors in the canyon from June 1 to October 1, largely to give the endangered bighorn sheep access to what little water there is.

In spring, however, the harsh desert breaks out in dune primroses and bright red ocotillo. Besides some feral horses and a few other invasive plants, such as tamarisk, the area has changed little over time.

From the park, the Anza Trail dips into Mexico, crosses the Colorado River back into the U.S. at Yuma, Arizona, then follows the Gila and Santa Cruz Rivers east and south. Interstate 8 steers along the same general route across the largely empty 230 miles to Tucson. At Tubac, where the expedition began, a state historic park displays the remains of the presidio, including the foundations, walls, and floor of the commandant's quarters. The local Anza Coalition is working on easements from property owners to put in a walking trail to the north.

In the meantime, a 4.5-mile trail running south to Tumacacori National Historical Park gives you a taste of Anza history. Paralleling and crossing over the Santa Cruz River, this trail was used by emigrants as they made their way from the mission at Tumacacori to the staging area at Tubac. Perhaps the best time to visit is during the Anza Days celebration in October. Up to 100 people, dressed as Spanish soldiers and settlers, take to the trail on horseback. Leading them as he has for the past ten years is historian Don Garate in the role of Juan Bautista de Anza. Says Garate, "Of all the historic trails this is probably the one people know the least about. There's a whole lot there, but it's in Spanish. Most of the history of the Southwest has been written by *gringos* who don't even speak the language."

Though warring Yuma Indians shut down the original Anza Trail in 1781, by then it had succeeded in bringing hundreds of settlers into California. Parts of this well-trod trail would be put into service in later years by ranchers, soldiers, forty-niners, and, of course, historic trail followers. ◆

During a clear night in California, stars dramatize the silhouette of palm trees in Anza-Borrego Desert State Park.

OVERMOUNTAIN VICTORY TRAIL

Shrouded in a blue haze, the ancient Blue Ridge Mountains of North
Carolina still appear much as they would have to the mountain men who rose up against the
British during the Revolutionary War.

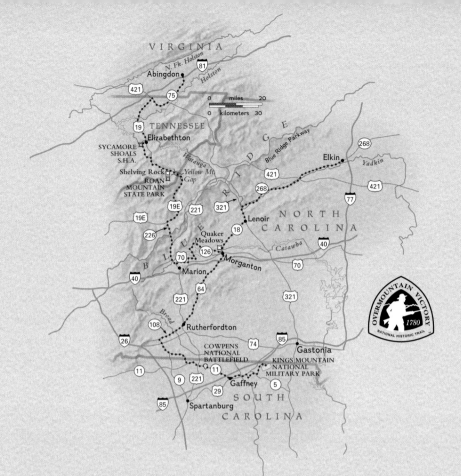

> *History...should place it beside Lexington and Bunker Hill...as one of the crucial engagements in our long struggle for independence.*
>
> —HERBERT HOOVER, 1930
> BATTLE ON KINGS MOUNTAIN

Sometimes history can turn on a few careless words. British Col. Patrick Ferguson was 36 years old in September 1780 when he sent a message to the "backwater men" of western North Carolina and eastern Tennessee during the middle of the American Revolutionary War. He told them that if they did not desist from their opposition to the British arms, he would march his army over the mountains, hang their leaders, and "lay their country waste with fire and sword." Tough words, and nearly his last— he would die the following month because

of them. Too late would he learn that you pay a price for threatening people who love their freedom.

The defeat of Ferguson at Kings Mountain in South Carolina was, according to Thomas Jefferson, "that turn of the tide of success" that led directly to Yorktown and victory in the Revolutionary War.

Ferguson never got a chance to march his army over the mountains; instead, the riled up "overmountain" men came marching after him. They started in Abingdon, Virginia, then headed south through the high country of Tennessee

A waterwheel sits beside a North Carolina mountain trail that shook with marching patriots in 1780.

and North Carolina, picking up men along the way so that by the time they were halfway to Kings Mountain, they numbered about 1,400. In two weeks, they covered some 220 rugged miles.

Earlier that year with the war stalled in the north, the British decided to sweep through the South recruiting loyalists and flushing out patriots. With their hold thus solidified, they could continue north and join with other forces to claim the Atlantic seaboard.

Modern-day patriots reenact the fierce battle that resulted in a defeat for the British at Kings Mountain in South Carolina.

The war had already divided communities and even families—some siding with the Crown, others with the rebellion. Britain's return to the area in 1780 only intensified the turmoil; outbreaks of burning, pillaging, murder, and torture rippled through the Carolinas. Britain underestimated the fierceness of the patriot resistance, though.

Ferguson and his militia of American-born loyalists served as the British western flank in the 1780 campaign. His fire-and-sword threat flushed out the patriots only too well. Up in the hills and hollows of the Holston and Watauga Rivers, mountain men grabbed their squirrel rifles and headed out, on foot and horseback, one militia

joining up with another. Living on the colonial frontiers practically beyond the reach of royal authority, these men were tough, self-reliant individuals. They were itching to make Ferguson eat his own words.

On September 25, the Overmountain Men mustered at Sycamore Shoals on the Watauga River, outside present-day Elizabethton, Tennessee. Eight years earlier this site had seen the birth of the Watauga Association, an early self-government established in defiance of England. The pioneers were so struck by the area's beauty—"mountains upon mountains upon mountains"—that they were not about to be dislodged by a kingdom an ocean away.

Today the Sycamore Shoals State Historic Area sits on the western edge of busy Elizabethton, seat of Carter County. Residents come here on nice weekends to picnic and to exercise on the shady trail that runs along the river. The river's babbling masks the noise of the nearby highway, making it easy to imagine the hundreds of marchers and horsemen in their hunting shirts and leggings, splashing across the shallows and gathering in the meadow at your back. Picture it as a massive rally, full of

A simple grave in the South Carolina forest at Kings Mountain National Military Park commemorates the death of Col. Patrick Ferguson, killed in battle by patriot backwoodsmen whom the arrogant colonel had dismissed as "mongrels."

loud bravado and whooping and egging each other on. Greetings and plans exchanged, these men were ready to head off to war.

A reconstruction of Fort Watauga and the film and exhibits in the visitor center help bring the story to life. Best of all, though, is to come here in September, when the Overmountain Victory Trail Association sponsors an annual re-creation of the muster and then the actual march. A core group of 8 to 15 people, many in period dress, will walk the whole way, while several dozen might join on any particular day.

"We camp as close as possible to the actual campsites and on the same dates,

rain or shine, we go. Rain didn't stop our ancestors 221 years ago," says grand marshall Allen Ray. Though shopping centers, towns, and highways have filled in parts of the original landscape, there are still some 50 miles of off-road trails, and the association is working to keep them preserved.

From Sycamore Shoals, the original Overmountain Men, led by Col. William Campbell, headed southeast 20 miles and camped near Shelving Rock, an overhang where they could keep their gunpowder dry. You can see this natural shelter on a curve in the road as you approach Roan Mountain State Park. The militia went around the

British commander Col. Patrick Ferguson brandishes his sword as he leads his loyalist troops on Kings Mountain.

Using the forest for cover the attacking patriots decimated the exposed loyalist force, killing some 388 of them.

Apple branches are heavy with fruit in Altapass, North Carolina, site of a mountain pass through the Blue Ridge that was used during colonial times. The orchard, planted in 1908, is open to the public.

north side of Roan Mountain, but by all means you should drive the ten-mile road that goes through the park and climbs to the mountaintop. The 6,285-foot-high peak supports a cold-climate, spruce-fir forest and affords spectacular views of the Appalachians rolling away in misty blue sequence.

The views have remained essentially unchanged in the past 220 years. Trails wind through grassy balds that have an unusual and little understood ecology thought to be caused by the grazing of prehistoric animals. Natural rhododendron gardens bloom lavishly in spring, while in late September (when the Overmountain Men came through the area) the forest begins to take on its autumn plumage.

The men went through Yellow Mountain Gap, the highest point on the trail at 4,682 feet. It snowed as they crossed, and two men lost their nerve and deserted to warn Ferguson of the patriot army's approach. Ferguson's reaction was to decamp from Gilbert Town (near Rutherfordton, North Carolina) and head east, perhaps in retreat or to find better ground. The patriots stepped up their speed to catch him.

In 1975 local citizens reenacted the march and began gathering thousands of signatures to petition Congress for official recognition of the trail. Five years later, on the bicentennial of the march, the Overmountain Victory Trail achieved national historic trail status. Today, you can walk the trail during the annual reenactment, or follow it on a commemorative auto route through approximately 300 miles of mostly rural countryside.

The auto route winds east on US 19 into North Carolina, then south through a handful of little mining towns that prospered briefly in the early 1900s. After crossing the Blue Ridge Parkway, the route follows winding backroads to Morganton, located halfway along the trail. A 70-mile branch of the trail joins the main route here; from the northwest, it mostly follows the Yadkin River, along which 350 troops marched to join the others at Quaker Meadows, now a fairground and golf course just west of Morganton. Though historic sites on this branch are few, it's a lovely spin through a pastoral countryside of hayfields, wildflowers, and fruit orchards.

South of Morganton on US 64, the scenery is much the same until Rutherfordton and the US 74 corridor. This is furniture, textile, and lumber country, part of a growing exurban sprawl across the Carolina Piedmont. But as the route approaches South Carolina, the pastoral scenery picks up again.

The old county courthouse sits in the town square of Morganton, North Carolina. Completed in 1837, it now serves as a museum.

Learning that Ferguson was on the move east, the patriots selected about 900 of their best horsemen to ride out in pursuit. They stopped for a quick supper at Cowpens in South Carolina, then pushed on. In a ferocious effort that had begun at dawn of that day, they made 50 miles in 36 hours, riding right up to Kings Mountain and into battle. Here Ferguson and his 1,100-man battalion decided to make a stand, crowing "We are kings of Kings Mountain!"

These self-proclaimed royals would soon be deposed. Named for a local settler instead of a monarch, the forested mountain is a Blue Ridge spur rising 150 feet from its surroundings. Normally a tactical advantage, the high ground in this case had a couple of disadvantages. First of all, the slopes in 1780 were covered with a virgin forest of tremendous poplars and oaks that made excellent cover for the backwoodsmen. Second, the top was a 600-yard-long bald that exposed the loyalists like so many ducks in a pen.

On the afternoon of October 7, the patriot forces encircled the base of the mountain and began working their way up. The muskets of the loyalists (accurate to

Snow blankets an orchard located along the Overmountain Victory Trail. While traveling through this area, the

patriot forces were slowed by a heavy snowstorm. Two disheartened members of the party fled to the British.

about 75 yards) were no match for the long rifles of the patriots, who were old hands at shooting game from 300 yards away. Ironically, Ferguson may have had the best piece on the field—a breechloading rifle of his own invention—but British conservatives had yet to appreciate its advantages.

The patriots, screeching like devils, kept driving up the mountain while taking advantage of the terrain's natural cover, fending off three bayonet charges, and coming on again.

Wheeling his horse and shrilling orders with a silver whistle, Ferguson made an especially easy target. A volley of bullets found their mark. The cocky British colonel fell dead. As his opponents cheered, his horse ran in panic, dragging his body across the battlefield with one foot still caught in its stirrup.

Loyalist survivors raised a white flag and called for surrender, but the enraged patriots kept killing and killing, mercilessly giving no quarter, or mercy, for several minutes until their leader, Colonel Campbell, could stop them. In an hour, the battle was over.

Kings Mountain ranks as one of the most one-sided battles in American history: The patriots suffered 90 casualties; the loyalists lost their entire force, including 388 casualties and 716 taken prisoner. A small detachment marched the prisoners to a Continental post at Hillsborough, pausing to hang nine leaders. Along the way all but 130 of the prisoners escaped: There were simply too many prisoners and too few guards. But it didn't matter—the loyalists had been severely punished and were now eager to head home to their families.

After their victory at Kings Mountain, many patriots would return to these meadows three months later to help the Continentals defeat a larger, better-trained force of British regulars commanded by Banastre ("Bloody Ban") Tarleton, who was loathed for his failure to give quarter. Cowpens National Battlefield commemorates this crucial link in a chain of southern patriot successes.

A walking trail at Kings Mountain National Military Park gives a feeling for the battle's original terrain. Thin trees and scraggly underbrush have replaced the virgin forest, but a few venerable giants remain—trees that were young in 1780. The trail winds to the top of the mountain, where stone monuments honor the fallen and the total victory achieved here by the patriots. The momentum of that victory lasted all the way to the final showdown a year later at Yorktown, Virginia.

In 1980 President Carter recognized the significance of the Campaign to Kings Mountain by signing a law designating the historical route. As surely as liberty was born at Lexington and Valley Forge, America was born at Kings Mountain. ♦

A rugged landscape unfurls from a rocky vantage point in Virginia. Patriotic mountain men once marched some 220 miles to defeat British forces.

CHAPTER 3

LEWIS & CLARK TRAIL

Near the Montana-Idaho border, blooming beargrass emerges from the forest floor. The shallow root system makes the perennial easily susceptible to damage from human encroachment.

*They were the first national heroes since the Revolutionary War,
genuine superstars of the post-war generation.*

—STEPHEN E. AMBROSE, 2000
Lewis and Clark: Voyage of Discovery

Lewis and Clark—just their names evoke the spirit of grand adventure. You can see them in a number of paintings and memorial sculptures, standing on some bluff in elkskin jackets and trail-made moccasins, one person with a telescope to his eye, the other with a rifle in hand, while Sacagawea crouches nearby. They led the Corps of Discovery, the military expedition that headed out from St. Louis in May 1804. It was a tentacle of the young United States, groping blindly westward to find out what lay in the vast new land holdings. The group returned more than two years later, bringing back a trove of knowledge that made them permanent heroes in the pantheon of American explorers.

Of all national historic trails, this one was blazed by the smallest group—a permanent party of 31 men plus a teenage girl and her infant son—thus it makes for the most cohesive story. Whereas the emigrant trails and others are filled with thousands of stories, the Lewis & Clark Trail is really one story, some 3,700 miles long.

With the 1803 Louisiana Purchase more than doubling the size of the nation, the time was right to send a party of explorers up the Missouri River, over the Rockies, and into the disputed Northwest Territory. President Thomas Jefferson wanted to find out once and for all if there was a good water route to the Pacific. (The fact that none existed did not diminish the importance of a trip that was also about flag waving and muscle flexing; about announcing our country's presence to the French and English fur traders in the north, the Spanish in the south, and the Indians in the interior.) And, like the early voyages to the moon in the 1960s, this trip was about science. What kinds of plants, animals, minerals, landforms, and native peoples

LEWIS AND CLARK
NATIONAL HISTORIC TRAIL

Missouri
Lake Sakakawea
LITTLE MISSOURI S.P.
Stanton • Washburn
Fort Mandan
N. DAK.
★ Bismarck
FORT ABRAHAM LINCOLN S.P.
Little Missouri

Lake Oahe
SOUTH DAKOTA
Pierre ★

Sioux Falls •

Lake Francis Case
Missouri
Sioux City •

NEBRASKA   IOWA

Camp Council Bluffs
Platte Omaha • Council Bluffs

★ Lincoln

0   miles   100
0   kilometers   150

St. Joseph •   MISSOURI   Mississippi ILLINOIS
Wood Camp
• St. Louis

KANSAS   • Kansas City   Missouri
★ Topeka   • Jefferson City

Below: *Accessible mainly by foot or horseback, Little Missouri State Park in South Dakota offers breathtaking views of the badlands. The Sioux called this region Mako Shika, or "where the lands break."*

were out there in the bigger-than-ever United States? Pushing against the frontiers, the public was hungry for this kind of information.

One thing that makes the Lewis and Clark story an American favorite is that it was a huge success. And a success against long odds. Only one man died, likely of appendicitis, which was untreatable at the time. Two men deserted and another was discharged for insubordination—all near the beginning of the trip. When you consider that 30 tough-as-nails outdoorsmen were traveling like a family for more than two years, waking up every day to some new backbreaking labor or life-threatening ordeal, it is amazing that the group stayed together, let alone made it to the Pacific and back. That they survived a litany of accidents, grizzly attacks, near drownings, starvation rations, and tense Indian situations was due to the skill and resourcefulness of Corps members. That they were able to complete the mission without any serious friction among each other is a credit to the outstanding leadership of Lewis and Clark.

Both leaders were native Virginians—William Clark born in 1770, Meriwether

Expedition member Sacagawea communicates with natives from the lower Columbia River. William Clark wrote that her presence "reconsiles all the Indians as to our friendly intentions."

Lewis four years later—and both had served together in the army. When newly elected President Jefferson asked Lewis to be his personal secretary in 1801, Jefferson was already thinking about grooming him for an expedition up the Missouri. An avid hunter and woodsman, Lewis spent the next few years boning up on geology, botany, zoology, and astronomy. When the President offered him command of the Corps of Discovery, Lewis chose his old friend Clark as co-commander. Clark's steady temperament and outgoing personality complemented Lewis's tendency toward introspection and moodiness. Both were brilliant in times of crisis, particularly in standoffs with Indians. Of course they made mistakes, but not ruinous ones. They supported each other better than most married couples, adapted to whatever the wilderness threw at them, and were uncommonly good at keeping up the spirits of their men.

More people than ever are following the trail blazed by Lewis and Clark—not just visiting an occasional site, but gearing whole family vacations around it. Long sections can be traced by foot, canoe, and

A solitary canoeist enjoys the spectacular sunset along the upper Missouri River in Montana's Charles M. Russell National Wildlife Refuge. The refuge includes more than a million acres and boasts abundant wildlife.

car, traveling over the same terrain and even at the same time of year as the original explorers. Although it traverses mostly private lands, the Lewis & Clark Trail is largely a river route, which means that if you are willing to boat—and cope with dams—you can follow most of the original trail; commercial outfitters run trips through some popular scenic areas. As with the other historic trails, this is a work in progress—new hiking, biking, and horseback riding segments are constantly opening up. For most travelers, an auto tour suffices; trail signs, silhouetting the explorers, guide you along the general route and to specific sites.

As the Lewis and Clark Bicentennial approaches, this trail attracts more and more visitors. "We love birthdays in this country," says Dick Williams, manager of the Lewis and Clark National Historic Trail. "So the bicentennial draws people out. And the trail has so much romance— it goes through a beautiful part of the country, it has adventure, encounters with Indians, and exploration. You put it all together and people say—wow, this would be a great two-week vacation." It lures hard-core history buffs as well as touring families—anyone hungry for a whiff of the real Lewis and Clark in a land little changed after 200 years.

Dawn casts a golden glow over an immense field of wheat near Lake Elwell, a reservoir on the Marias River in

northern Montana. While exploring the river in 1806, the explorers skirmished with eight Blackfeet Indians.

Snow covers a reconstructed Mandan earth lodge at On-A-Slant Indian Village in North Dakota's Fort Abraham Lincoln State Park. Effigies of buffalo were placed on long poles in front of medicine lodges to bring good fortune.

The farther west you travel toward the Rockies on the Lewis & Clark National Historic Trail today, the more pristine the scenery grows; beyond those mountains, the landscape gradually becomes more civilized as you approach the Pacific.

Near what is now Council Bluffs, Iowa, the Corps of Discovery had its first parley with Indians—a group of Oto and Missouri—on August 3, 1804. In what would become a ritual, Lewis delivered a long speech, after which the captains handed out medallions, paint, breechcloths, gunpowder, balls, and whiskey. Then came a show of force—Lewis shot his gun in the air and displayed an array of scientific instruments.

Today, the river near Council Bluffs has shifted about three miles east of where it was in Lewis and Clark's day; forest fills in what was then a bare bluff top. But along much of the lower Missouri there are plenty of parks and wildlife refuges where you still can get a feel for the original terrain—floodplain forests and high-grass prairies interspersed with copses of wild berries.

The river itself, though channeled by the U.S. Army Corps of Engineers in the early 1900s, remains in many ways essentially the same wide, turbid, swift avenue it was in 1804. Numerous stretches are quiet, frequented by wild birds and lined by willows and cottonwoods. Outside of its towns, you can still stand on the banks and imagine a party of men working their keelboat and pirogues upstream, peering around the next bend for what might be there.

North Dakota, Montana, and Idaho contain the most interesting parts of the Lewis and Clark saga, as well as the most unaltered scenery. On their first winter out, the Corps built a fort near a cluster of Mandan villages just downriver from present-day Stanton, North Dakota. For five brutally cold months they lived among the Indians, took part in their games and dances, hunted with them, shared their women, and filled up pages of journals about what they experienced. We tend to think of Lewis and Clark constantly slogging west. But sometimes they would go miles out of their way just to check a route; in other cases, they had to just sit and wait.

Picture a scene by firelight—the mix of languages, the sound of a fiddle off in the shadows, the smells of tobacco and cooking meat, the faces of people wearing fringed leggings and warm buffalo robes—while outside the fort and the earth lodges a bitter wind wails across the open plains. To provision themselves during that long winter, the men would go hunting—by foot or borrowed horses—sometimes for more than a week. The Indians with their bows and arrows proved the better hunters and equestrians. With herds of bison streaming like freeway traffic down the hills and hollows— any one of the Corps' routine hunting trips would be the adventure of a lifetime today.

From the Indian point of view, the Lewis and Clark story has been far less upbeat.

Gerard Baker, superintendent of the Lewis and Clark Historic Trail, and himself a Mandan-Hidatsa, says, "Some tribes look at Lewis and Clark as the beginning of the end. A lot of them have very bitter stories. Although they see economic and cultural benefits of the bicentennial, they've been a bit reluctant to get involved. But we're stressing that this is a commemoration, not a celebration. The tribes are becoming involved— looking at their cultural and natural resources, at what they can show people— but in a lot of cases they're still skeptical."

Though Lewis and Clark generally treated Indians fairly, they were the vanguard of white settlement—after them came the deluge. In 1804, settlement was a thing of the East; the West was a matter of adventure. There were easier ways to make a buck than signing on with Lewis and Clark; you did it because there wasn't going to be another such opportunity—in all of history.

These days on the Lewis & Clark Trail, adventure involves the imagination—which reconstructions of Fort Mandan and a Mandan lodge help fuel. Wide swaths of grassy plains, a herd of bison, and the excellent exhibits at the Lewis and Clark Interpretive Center, all in or near the small town of Washburn, help too. David Borlaug, who heads the Interpretive Center and serves as president of the North Dakota Lewis & Clark Bicentennial Foundation, claims that "Lewis and Clark are changing the fact that North Dakota is the least visited state in the country. Since the center opened in 1997, rarely have we had less than 22 states represented by visitors on any given day. The recent publicity and the bicentennial ratchet up the attention, and now an infrastructure is being built. Interpretive centers like ours are popping up all along the trail."

In fact, the trail may have become too easy to follow; now the challenge lies mostly in taking time to fully appreciate it. Consider, for example, the 149-mile ribbon of water in Montana called the Upper Missouri National Wild and Scenic River. Gliding past a gorgeous panorama of white sandstone bluffs, rock pinnacles, and jumbled badlands, the river along this stretch gave Lewis and Clark their first views of the distant snow-crowned Rockies. Today it is one of the best places to experience the wilderness that the Corps of Discovery knew; you merely paddle downstream, having first decided to spend a few nights or a week outdoors. In the summer of 1805, Lewis and Clark had a much tougher time—they were heading upstream. And on their return the following year, there was little chance to admire the scenery: After a fight with some Blackfeet, in which two Indians were killed, Lewis and a small group were hurrying to rendezvous with Clark.

Though far from the beaten path, the stretch from Fort Benton to Kipp State Park has grown in popularity with canoeists and rafters. In 1995, there were 2,760 floaters registered; four years later that number had nearly doubled. "People that have been coming for years and years definitely think it has gotten more crowded," says Sandra Padilla, river ranger at the Bureau of Land Management in Lewistown. "But there are days, especially in the off-season, when you can still put in on the river and find a lot of solitude." The entire 149 miles is crossed by only two small bridges and two ferries. Other than that, you can hardly find the hand of man here. The animal population has changed in the past two centuries—grizzlies, bison, and Audubon bighorn sheep are gone—but songbirds, deer, elk, and great blue herons are still plentiful.

And the Great Falls of the Missouri still exist. This series of five, heart-pounding cascades in western Montana—the highest nearly 90 feet—blocked the Lewis and Clark party for a whole month. Rapturous descriptions of "one of the most beautiful objects in nature" soon gave way to the most grueling work of their trip yet—portaging six, 1,000-pound dugout canoes and tons of gear 18 miles around the falls. The way was carpeted with cactus that punctured double-thick buffalo-hide moccasins. Add the torments of mosquitoes, flash floods, seven-inch-diameter hail, grizzlies, and buffalo bulls and you have some idea of the original portage. Astonishingly, Clark was able to report that "notwith standing all this dificuelty they go with great chearfulness." Today, to follow the exact same route, you'd have to cut across a wheat field, an Air Force base, and the southeastern part of Great Falls city. In other words, it can't be done. But the falls still roar and the city holds several noteworthy sites steeped in trail lore.

Sporting a shaggy coat, daggerlike horns, and a quizzical look, a mountain goat perches on a rocky ledge in Montana. Particularly active in mornings and evenings, these agile mammals can inhabit steep mountain cliffs.

The expedition pushed over the Continental Divide and beyond the boundaries of the Louisiana Purchase at Lemhi Pass, between what are now Montana and Idaho. Lewis wrote of the "immence ranges of high mountains," crossed the Divide, and drank from a cold, clear creek, exultant that at last he was tasting water that flowed to the Pacific. He and his comrades were the first whites in this region, largely untamed even today. A 15-mile-long, gravel-and-dirt road tops out at 7,373 feet. It remains a moment to savor— the clear mountain air, the sagebrush and wildflowers at your feet, and the ranks of pleated mountains running to the horizons both east and west.

With horses bartered from the Shoshoni, Lewis and Clark then veered sharply north for some 150 miles, looking for a way through the Bitterroot Range. The pack-laden horses had to pick their way across steep, talus slopes covered with sharp rocks. Several animals fell, others simply gave out. By mid-September, the Corps was heading west over the Lolo Trail, an old Nez Perce route connecting the Columbia Basin with the northern plains. Low on food, they had to hurry before winter began. Ahead lay 170 miles of the most rugged land they had

Stretching more than four miles, the Astoria-Megler Bridge connects the states of Oregon and Washington.

The Lewis and Clark expedition built Fort Clatsop nearby and encamped there for the winter of 1805-1806.

yet faced—a forbidding labyrinth of peaks clad with dense forest. Even with the Indian guide they had picked up at the Divide, it was a superhuman struggle to keep on track. Scarce game meant they had to eat their horses, rationing the meat to prevent starvation; snow began falling—and morale along with it. Who would have the guts during such misery to sit down and describe a new bird and a new species of honeysuckle? Time and again, Lewis stayed focused on his job on days that would have brought a lesser man to his knees.

Spanning the ridges above the Lochsa River, Idaho's Lolo Motorway may sound like a high-speed invitation to take in the magnificent scenery Lewis and Clark were too weary to enjoy. In fact, it's some 100 miles of the hairiest driving you're likely to encounter on the whole trail. Surveyed in the 1860s to handle gold-rush traffic, the route was used in 1877 by the Nez Perce on their flight from the U.S. Army—hence it's also part of the Nez Perce National Historic Trail. It remains a primitive, narrow, jolting, dirt road with fanglike rocks and headlight-smashing limbs that vexes even high-clearance vehicles. Since uphill drivers have the right of way, motorists sometimes back up as much as a quarter mile, along sheer drop-offs, to find a passing place. Those who complete this two-to-three-day, sweaty-palm adventure may be tempted to think Lewis and Clark had it easy. On the other hand, there are several gentle stretches, as well as beckoning meadows and creek sides that practically echo with the explorers' footsteps.

After making it to the mouth of the Columbia on the present-day border of Oregon and Washington, the Corps of Discovery holed up for the winter a few miles from the south bank. It rained 94 of the 106 days; the fleas were bad; the food was meager; colds and rheumatism were rampant. "Not any occurrences today worthy of notice," was the typical log entry. Set in a grove of sitka spruce, Fort Clatsop National Memorial keeps Lewis and Clark fans from suffering the same end-of-trail anticlimax. Redolent with wood smoke and elk hides, the expert reconstruction of the fort is so convincing you almost get déjà vu. Costumed interpreters wander about; water drips into rain barrels (it still rains constantly); and at the canoe landing rough-hewn dugouts are ready to launch.

The explorers made it back to St. Louis the following September. No wonder they had been given up for dead—there had been no news from them since they left Fort Mandan nearly a year and a half earlier. Journeying more than 8,000 miles, they returned with descriptions of some 300 new plants and animals. They had met dozens of Indian tribes. And they had drawn the first lines on a blank map of the American West. For all this, and for surviving with such style, we salute them today. Their status as American heroes seems ensured for a long time to come. ◆

Moss seems to burst from the walls of a narrow passageway in the Columbia River Gorge— an ancient river canyon that cuts through the Cascade Mountain Range.

CHAPTER 4

SANTA FE
TRAIL

In the Kiowa National Grasslands of New Mexico, the road trails off into an endless vista of
prairie. Enterprising 19th-century traders traveled between Missouri and Santa Fe—some 800
miles, much of it over landscape like this—in ox-drawn wagons.

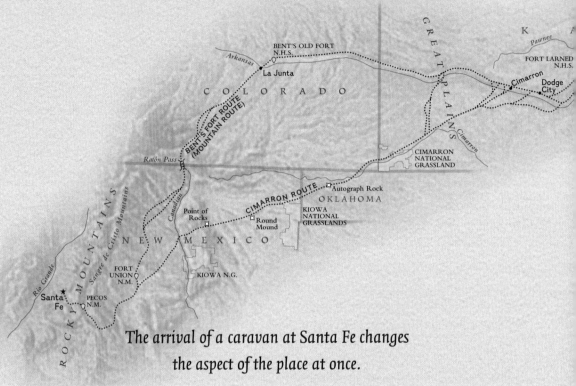

The arrival of a caravan at Santa Fe changes the aspect of the place at once.

—Josiah Gregg, 1831

When William Becknell and his small band of travelers stumbled into Santa Fe from the Rocky Mountains in 1821 with wares to sell, they had no idea what they had started. A few entrepreneurs over the years had risked jail sentences by defying Spain's iron grip over New Mexico and slipping through the borders to bring in foreign trade goods. The unlucky ones ended up in prison. But a few months before Becknell's arrival, New Mexico had gained its independence from Spain and ended the old trade sanctions that prohibited U.S. traders from selling goods there. Becknell may have taken a calculated risk, guessing he would be favorably received. At any rate, he quickly sold the trade goods he'd brought and returned to Missouri with rawhide bags full of silver coins. The Santa Fe Trail was open.

When you think of the Santa Fe Trail, think commerce, not settlement; think shrewd traders, not greenhorn pioneer families. Instead of converted farm vehicles, think of big, brand-new Conestoga wagons with red wheels, blue bodies, and white covers pulled by parades of oxen up to ten yokes long. And think of Mexican merchants rolling east as much as Americans going west. Within its first year of operation, the

In 1874 a white man sits atop a pile of buffalo skins. Such sights enraged Plains Indians and helped foment violence.

Silhouetted against billowing clouds, an iron sculpture near Council Grove, Kansas, depicts a covered wagon and horseman on the Santa Fe Trail. In 1825, the Osage Indians allowed passage through their lands for the trail.

trail was doing a $15,000 business. By 1835, the total value of trade was $140,000. In 1860 it was $3.5 million—about $53 million in today's dollars. The sudden success of the Santa Fe Trail as a trade corridor was simple. Mexico had the raw goods the United States sorely needed—silver, wool, furs, mules. And the United States had the manufactured goods Mexico wanted—everything from printed cotton and playing cards to tools and mirrors. The Santa Fe-Missouri connection was a market waiting to happen. After 1821, the only barrier was geography—800 miles of prairie and plains.

Anything could occur on that eight-week wagon journey, and that's where the legends were made—tales of wild storms, flooded rivers, buffalo stampedes, dry heat that shrank wooden wheels from their iron rims, and attacks by Indians. Interspersed among long days of dust, mud, and mosquitoes, the adventures were like nuggets the old-timers could take out and polish after the Santa Fe Trail had become obsolete.

When the railroad pushed into Santa Fe in 1880, the trail became a memory, the province of wind and rain, prairie dogs and jackrabbits. In 1987 it was designated a national historic trail in honor of its importance as an avenue of early economic expansion and cultural exchange. About 90 percent of it now lies on private land, but a signed auto route angles through the same landscape. Though farms have replaced much of the original tall- and short-grass prairies, the region remains largely rural, and many of the same streams, rock formations, and other natural landmarks appear as they did in the mid-1800s. By car, foot, horse, and bicycle, modern travelers can take segments of the trail back to a time when the pace of business was measured not in light-speed transactions but in distances you could walk, not in electronic accounts but in coins you could hold in your hands.

The trail began at Missouri River ports, where steamboats could load and unload goods. Independence, Missouri, became the main eastern terminal, its docks and dirt streets a constant polyglot hubbub of activity. Writer Francis Parkman observed the scene in 1846: "There was an incessant hammering and banging from a dozen blacksmiths' sheds, where the heavy wagons were being repaired, and the horses and oxen shod. The streets were thronged with men, horses, and mules."

Nowadays, Independence still bustles, though it has become a suburb of Kansas City. Its quiet historic district holds a dozen or so buildings from the trail days, including the Bingham-Waggoner estate, erected by a Santa Fe Trail merchant in 1852 and currently one of a handful of old properties open to the public. A prior owner complained about the noise and dust from the trail—really a wide road—which went along the east and south sides of the estate.

Another resident, George Caleb Bingham, was a famous painter of frontier life, though little remains here from his time. Nineteen acres of grounds set this rambling house off from the surrounding neighborhood, enough to get you started in the Santa Fe Trail time machine.

The clincher lies in a field out back—in 1999, a set of wagon swales was discovered here. Created by freight wagons and oxen hooves, swales and ruts were enhanced by erosion. You'll find plenty of people along the trail today who claim to have ruts on their property, but in urban areas ruts are an increasing rarity. Across the street, the National Frontier Trails Center has a number of interesting exhibits from the Santa Fe, Oregon, and California Trails, all of which used Independence as a jumping-off point. Among the thousands of books, maps, diaries, and letters housed here in the country's largest overland trail library is a journal found in a dump in 1985. It was written by a 16-year-old girl during her 1866 journey to California. Such items, says John Mark Lamberton, Director of the National Frontier Trail Center, are constantly surfacing.

From Independence the Santa Fe Trail hooked southwest into the Flint Hills of eastern Kansas; US 56 roughly follows it today. Unlike the emigrant trails, which were grassroots movements, the Santa Fe was sanctioned by the government from the start. The federal government surveyed it in the mid-1820s and built forts to protect the trade. Government agents also negotiated

Women and children rest while traveling by covered wagon through what is now New Mexico. The

Santa Fe Trail paved the way for others to follow, including gold seekers and land-hungry emigrants.

right-of-way treaties with local Indians, most prominently at Council Grove, Kansas, in 1825. Agreements made here with Osage chiefs, in a grove of trees, helped keep the eastern half of the trail relatively safe.

Still a small town, Council Grove was the last outfitting place on the trail, the final chance to cut trees for firewood and spare axles. Entering town from the east, you can see what remains of the original council oak, enshrined under a shelter on the right side of the road. A windstorm toppled it in 1958, but there are several other trees around town, marked with plaques, from the trail era. A block west stands a striking statue of a pioneer mother staring resolutely west; she wears a bonnet and sturdy boots, holds an infant in one arm and a walking stick in the other, while another child clings to her skirts. The Daughters of the American Revolution (DAR) put up a dozen of these 10-foot-tall stone memorials in the early 1900s, including four on the Santa Fe Trail, even though it was not primarily a pioneer route. The DAR, in fact, is responsible for more than 100 stone markers on this trail alone— the earliest and most comprehensive such effort to commemorate the Santa Fe Trail.

A 19th-century man examines the names inscribed in Pawnee Rock, a tall point on the Santa Fe Trail that rose some 50 feet above the Kansas prairie.

Near the pioneer mother, Main Street crosses the gentle Neosho River at approximately the same shallow ford where wagon caravans crossed. The town has since put in a walkway along the river and some interpretive signs; you can easily imagine the wagons and livestock edging down the gentle banks and splashing across the rocky-bottomed river. The nearby Hays House restaurant, a national historic landmark, dates from 1857 and still serves bountiful country fare in an unpretentious setting.

About halfway along the trail, in southwestern Kansas, Fort Larned was built in 1859 to protect wagons and mail coaches. It became a staging post for battles against the Indians and a distribution center for treaty "annuities"—handouts of clothing, tobacco, and food to local tribes. Intended to mollify the Indians, the annuities actually made them dependent upon the government and failed to achieve a lasting peace. Now a national historic site, Fort Larned boasts nine original sandstone buildings and a restored parade ground. But what most recaptures the period is a piece of restored prairie on a bend in the Pawnee River. At the nearby rut site, wagon swales furrow ground pocked by prairie dogs; both contribute to the look of yesterday.

An underground Pueblo Indian ceremonial chamber, or kiva, lies in the foreground, while the ruins of an 18th-century Spanish mission church are seen in the distance at Pecos National Monument in New Mexico. Established as an Anasazi pueblo in 1300, at its height the Indian village boasted some 700 rooms built around an interior plaza. Decimated over the years by Indian raids and disease, the final residents left in 1838.

About five days' travel beyond Fort Larned, the wagon trains had a choice: Cross the Arkansas River into what was then Mexican territory, then, using a compass, pick their way across 60 miles of waterless sage country to the Cimarron River. Or, take the Bent's Fort Route, also known as the Mountain Route, into the mountains of southeastern Colorado. Most travelers, at least in the early years, opted for the quicker, easier Cimarron Route. The two weeks saved, though, sometimes came at a price. The lack of water could spell disaster, and, as the years went by and the buffalo were depleted, the Indians grew increasingly hostile.

Whereas Indian raids on the emigrant trails were overstated, here they were frequent. The trains of mules and horses became irresistible to tribes that had old scores to settle with a seemingly endless caravan of whites. Though most caravans got by with little or no trouble, the ones that didn't made headlines. Along the Cimarron River, Comanches killed famous mountain man Jedediah Smith in 1831 on his first Santa Fe Trail trip. According to a Mexican trader, Smith killed one of the Indians first, though the whole story will probably never be known.

Tucked in the southwestern corner of Kansas, the Cimarron National Grassland is

Sunlight glints off the gaily painted wheels of a freight wagon at Bent's Old Fort in Colorado. Used on the

Santa Fe Trail, creaking behemoths like this one were stuffed to the roof with up to 6,000 pounds of goods.

perhaps the best place on the entire trail for experiencing the original terrain of the route. Some 23 miles of the trail, the longest stretch on public land, thread this rippling grassland. To keep the swales from being eroded away, a parallel hiking and bridle trail runs most of the distance, sometimes crossing over the old ruts. Through a short-grass ecosystem speckled with wildflowers, the trail stays within hailing distance of the cottonwoods lining the Cimarron River; red-winged blackbirds *chir* in the underbrush, while the wind hissing through the grass sounds like the ocean. Deer, antelope, and rattlesnakes still live here, and distant cattle can look almost like a herd of buffalo.

The Cimarron Route clips the southwestern corner of Colorado, then the panhandle of Oklahoma, before proceeding into New Mexico. It passes such landmarks as Autograph Rock, where Mexicans and Americans carved their names in sandstone, and the aptly named Round Mound. You have to drive ten miles of dirt-and-gravel roads to reach Point of Rocks, but the excursion is worth it. Rising 280 feet from the floor of a mesa, this granite outcrop had a good spring that made it attractive to travelers. It was also, unfortunately, a great place for Indians to lie in ambush. Possibly belonging to victims of violence, the dozen graves here are a stark reminder of the risks international traders took in the mid-1800s. Point of Rocks is one of the few privately owned sites open to the public. The Gaines family has lived here

since 1898 and continues to welcome visitors free of charge. "Until the day comes when someone abuses the privilege," says Fay Gaines, "we will keep it open."

The trail continues southwest, to the Sangre de Cristo Mountains and Santa Fe. On August 18, 1846, Gen. Stephen Kearny and his 1,700-man Army of the West, having traversed the Santa Fe Trail at lightning speed, marched north from Apache Canyon through arroyos and sagebrush flats into the plaza of Santa Fe. The American flag went up over the palace of governors without a shot being fired— apart from a celebratory fanfare of artillery and bugles. New Mexico was now American soil, and although a year and a half of sporadic bloodshed would follow, in effect the Santa Fe Trail was no longer an international trail. No matter—the commerce of the trail marched to its own oxen-hoofed beat. It was profits and losses the merchants cared about, not whose flag flew in the plaza.

In the busy, touristy, still-very-commercial heart of Santa Fe today, the low, thick-walled adobe palace continues to command the north side of the plaza, where Pueblo Indians still sell their wares. The buying and selling is brisk in the surrounding shops. It's business as usual here at the western end of the Santa Fe Trail. ♦

At the Trade Room in Bent's Old Fort, Indians would barter four buffalo robes for a single, colorful, red blanket.

TRAIL
OF
TEARS

The sun sets beyond the scarlet-streaked ridges of the Great Smoky Mountains. In the 1800s, about 1,000 Cherokee fled to these densely-forested mountains on the North Carolina-Tennessee border to escape forced relocation by the U.S. government.

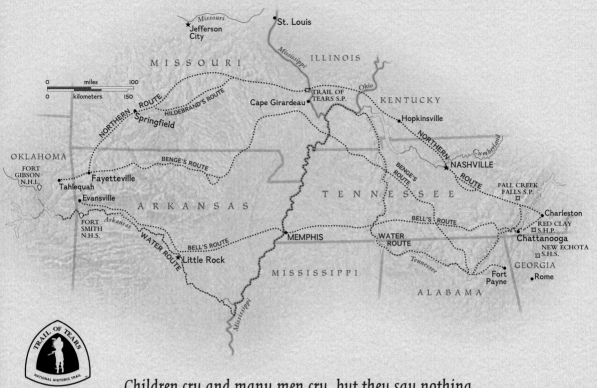

Children cry and many men cry, but they say nothing
and just put their heads down and keep on.

—A SURVIVOR, 1800s

Not all of our historic trails recall a celebratory chapter in the nation's history. While Native Americans appear in the stories of almost all the trails, they usually act as supporting cast—helping or hindering the progress of white settlement. On the two national historic trails in which Indians are the lead characters—the Nez Perce trail and the Trail of Tears—settlement is again the issue, but from the Indian point of view. Both of these trails commemorate heartrending episodes, yet they touch us in different ways.

The Nez Perce story was about a small band of renegade warriors and their families who were trying to escape the U.S. Army in the West. The Trail of Tears, on the other hand, was composed of nearly 16,000 evicted landowners, huddling in blankets as they walked or rode some 800 miles from the southeastern states to Oklahoma.

During the Trail of Tears, between 1830 and 1850, an estimated 100,000 Choctaws, Chickasaws, Creeks, Cherokee, and Seminoles were forced from their homelands to the new "Indian Territory" beyond the Mississippi. Though all these Indian nations suffered from the Indian Removal Act of 1830, the actual Trail of Tears, or "Trail Where They Cried," was the one traveled by the Cherokee during a massive migration in the fall and winter of 1838-39. The modern

Plunging 256 feet into a shaded pool, Tennessee's Fall Creek Falls is the highest waterfall east of the Rockies.

trail traces three major land routes and one water route. Though highway development has altered much of the land along the route and 98 percent of the land is privately owned, there are several sites of historic interest that travelers may still visit.

What the white settlers in the early 1800s wanted from the Indians was land. At the time of the American Revolution, Cherokee territory included most of Tennessee, Georgia, and Kentucky—and parts of South Carolina, Virginia, West Virginia, Mississippi, and Alabama. By 1820, after dozens of treaties, their land was down to 10 percent of its original size. Cherokee spokesman Major Ridge put it this way: "I know the Indians have an older title than the white man. We obtained the land from the living God above, yet they are strong and we are weak. We are few, they are many."

It was the discovery of gold at Dahlonega in 1829 that brought things to a head. The state of Georgia declared that they would secede from the Union if all Indians in the South were not relocated west of the Mississippi. To make it easier for whites to displace the Cherokee, the Georgia legisla-

Dressed in traditional garb, native women celebrate the annual powwow in Hopkinsville, Kentucky. Cherokee ancestors once camped nearby during their forced relocation to the West.

ture simply declared the Cherokee government null; furthermore, Cherokee were not allowed to mine, hold meetings, or testify against whites in court. The state then began holding lotteries to distribute Cherokee land to white newcomers.

But the Cherokee were not going to take this lying down. By 1830, they had their own newspaper, printed in both English and a written form of Cherokee developed in the 1820s by Sequoyah; many of them were partially white and lived in small houses with white picket fences; some operated plantations and even owned slaves. They laid down their own law: The Cherokee who gave up land without consent of the tribal council would pay with their lives. Meanwhile, they took the case to the U.S. courts. Delivering a speech in New York in 1832, John Ridge (Major Ridge's son) said, "You asked us to throw off the hunter and warrior state—we did so. You asked us to form a republican government—we did so. You asked us to cultivate the earth and learn the mechanical arts—we did so. You asked us to cast away our idols and worship your God—we did so."

A rock along the Trail of Tears exhibits grooves that were used to collect the resin produced by burning pine branches. Travelers used the viscous pine pitch to lubricate wheel axles.

That same year, the Supreme Court ruled that Georgia's laws against the Cherokee were unconstitutional. Yet President Jackson refused to enforce the ruling of the highest court in the land, maintaining that it was "absurd" to think that a sovereign nation could operate independently within the United States. In his opinion, the Indians had "neither the intelligence, the industry, the moral habits nor the desire of improvement which are essential to any favorable change in their condition."

In 1835, 20 Cherokee signed a treaty at New Echota, Georgia, agreeing their nation would move in exchange for five million dollars—which was never paid. None of the signers were elected officials; and even though 15,000 people signed a petition stating that their treaty had been made by an unauthorized minority, the U.S. Congress ratified it by one vote.

Not believing that they would really be forced from their homes, the vast majority of Cherokee stayed put. Finally in May 1838, the deadline came and soldiers began going door to door, some of them behaving with brutality. Individuals were given no time to collect possessions or locate family members; those who resisted were beaten or put in chains; the old and infirm were pushed out at bayonet point; women were molested. Waiting like wolves, hordes of plunderers moved in as the

A spider busily constructs its web near a river in Tahlequah, Oklahoma. After being deported from

their homeland, the surviving Cherokee chose Tahlequah as their nation's permanent capital in 1839.

Forced to leave their homes, Cherokee men, women, and children march along the aptly named Trail of Tears. "Long time we travel on way to new land, many days pass and people die very much," one survivor recalled.

wagons rolled away. Wrote one soldier: "I fought through the Civil War and have seen men shot to pieces and slaughtered by the thousands, but the Cherokee removal was the cruelest work I ever knew."

More than 16,000 Cherokee were herded into stockades—disease-ridden concentration camps that claimed many lives. Some groups were moved west in the summer, but drought and sickness took a toll. Most were allowed to wait until fall when they could head out under their own guidance. Heavy rains slowed their progress, and then came a bitter winter. Ice floes on the Mississippi bogged down some groups on the east side for weeks. Women tried to gather edible plants from the forest to sup-

plement inadequate rations of white flour and old salt pork, yet many of the plants were unfamiliar. Death from malnutrition and exposure became commonplace. Most families lost at least one member. In all, some 4,000 Cherokee died—nearly a fifth of their entire population.

One army captain wrote, "Upwards of a thousand Indians passed by today…. I could not help but think that some fearful retribution would yet come upon us from this injured race."

In the town of Rome in northwestern Georgia, the Chieftains Museum occupies the former home of Cherokee leader Major John Ridge. A ferryboat and plantation owner, Ridge built this gracious mansion around an existing log cabin. Now a national historic landmark, the house displays a number of archaeological artifacts and exhibits that tell the story of Major Ridge. Debby Brown, with Cherokee ancestry, bright red hair, a country twang, and an infectious enthusiasm for local history, brings the tale to life. "They were a neat family, because they were able to stand with one foot in each society—Indian and white—and do it well." Though Debby's great-great-grandmother was a full-blooded Cherokee, she pretended she was white so she could stay in Georgia. Not until 1962, in a gesture of reconciliation, did Georgia repeal the deportation law.

Long shadows lend a ghostly aura to the early 1800s Tennessee cabin that once belonged to the Cherokee leader Tekahskeh.

A short distance north, in cattle- and chicken-producing Gordon County, the New Echota State Historic Site commemorates the village that served as the Cherokee capital from 1825 to 1838. You can wander among reconstructed and original buildings that give an idea of how far the Cherokee had gone to adapt to white culture. The council house, supreme courthouse, print shop, tavern, and middle-class farmstead look as any 19th-century pioneer village did. It was here in 1835 that the Treaty of New Echota was signed, trading away all Cherokee lands east of the Mississippi River; less than three years later the removal began. Today the peacefulness of this rural site belies the unsettled times it memorializes. Perhaps most telling is an 1832 survey line, dividing into parcels what was still Cherokee property. You can imagine the impatience of settlers waiting to move in on what they considered theirs. The Cherokee newspaper called it "Robbery!"

To the north, just across the Tennessee line, Red Clay served as a kind of capital in exile after Georgia banned all Cherokee political meetings. Eleven major councils, attended by thousands, were held here in the few years before the Trail of Tears. Smaller than New Echota, this state historical area centers on a limpid spring called Blue Hole, which the Cherokee considered sacred. Fields and woods edge the reconstructed buildings, and a nature trail offers a hint of the area's early 1800s appearance.

About 1,000 Cherokee managed to escape the roundup in the mountains of North Carolina and Tennessee. Today their descendants, numbering over 13,000, make up the Eastern Band of the Cherokee. Their headquarters is the

Expressive Cherokee ceremonial masks are displayed at the Oconaluftee Village in Cherokee, North Carolina. Used

by men in the ceremony known as the *Booger Dance*, such masks were carved out of buckeye, basswood, or gourds.

tourist town of Cherokee, just south of Great Smoky Mountains National Park in North Carolina.

As they have since the 1920s, Cherokee "chiefs" still make good money here posing in Plains Indian regalia in front of trading posts. Ironically, the older, more authentic Cherokee history is preserved in a slick, new museum—high-tech audio and video effects relate the Cherokee story as you follow a winding path through low-lit galleries. The nearby Oconaluftee Indian Village, opened in 1952, provides a glimpse of 18th-century Cherokee life. Watching demonstrations of basketry, flint knapping, and canoe-making is instructive, but it's just as fascinating to talk to these costumed, but real, Cherokee about their current lives. You learn, for example, that the Cherokee language and history are far from dead—since 1985 they have been required courses at the local high school.

About halfway along the northern route, Trail of Tears State Park in southeastern Missouri occupies a forested bluff at the site of a crucial Mississippi river crossing. It was here that hundreds of Indians had to wait for ice to clear during the winter of 1838-39; dozens perished in or near what is now the park. One of the few mid-route commemorations of the Trail of Tears, this scenic park is also a winter roosting site for bald eagles.

The end of the trail was the beginning of the Cherokee's new life. In 1849, they began rebuilding their government in Tahlequah, Oklahoma. Situated in the foothills of the Ozarks, Tahlequah today is an unassuming town of about 10,000 people, home to Northeastern State University and the Cherokee Nation. In the heart of town, the old Cherokee National Capitol Building, dating from 1870, is now used for tribal court proceedings; the two-story, brick building stands a block north of the 1845 Cherokee Supreme Court Building, currently undergoing restoration.

Just south of town, the Cherokee Heritage Center holds a museum and an Indian village similar to the one in Cherokee, though on a smaller scale. One life-size sculptural installation depicts nine ghostly figures on foot or crouching by fallen loved ones; a wind moans, and voices tell sad stories. One survivor remembered the quietness of the trail, the only sounds footsteps and an occasional cough.

"I will laugh no more while living," another said, "but when new land is reached in skies and all my people meet me again, then I make joyful laugh."

We honor the Trail of Tears to remember, and to learn. It teaches us that the path of American history was blazed by more than one group, and that the wrong turns should never be forgotten. ♦

The rushing waters of Missouri's Pickle Creek create an idyllic setting. In January 1839, the nearby Mississippi River was icebound, making the Cherokee crossing into Missouri treacherous.

OREGON TRAIL

A placid stretch of the Columbia River belies the adventure many emigrants endured. An 1852 diarist described a turbulent trip down the river: "Waves washed over the canoe and as high as my head completely drenching us." One companion screamed throughout.

Where shall we find room for all our people, unless we have Oregon?

—Representative Andrew Kennedy,
Indiana, 1844

You've been heading west for some 500 miles, tramping alongside an ox-drawn wagon across the woodlands and prairies of Kansas and eastern Nebraska, on the road for 40 days. You find yourself wishing for a hill, anything to relieve the tedium of a land so flat it makes you feel like a bug on a billiard table. Finally you make it to Windlass Hill, in western Nebraska. You're staring down 300 feet of a rutted incline that looks almost perpendicular. You and your companions lock the wagons' wheels and ease them down with ropes. Horses have died here, wagons have crashed. You've heard stories: "Horses dashing furiously with the pieces down the hills and precipices—the noise,

dust and confusion, the men shouting, and women screaming." Somehow you make it into Ash Hollow, where there's a cool spring and shade trees and several other parties with tents already pitched. . . .

Or, you've been driving all day in your air-conditioned sedan, dogging the emigrant trail along the Platte River. When it breaks from the interstate to follow the North Platte you go with it, more or less, up US 26. You get out and walk to the top of Windlass Hill, probably with the whole place to yourself, and you look around at the rocky hills and sage-lined gullies, the wind whispering through sun-tipped grasses and purple penstemons. You hear the song of a meadowlark caught in a big silence. At last

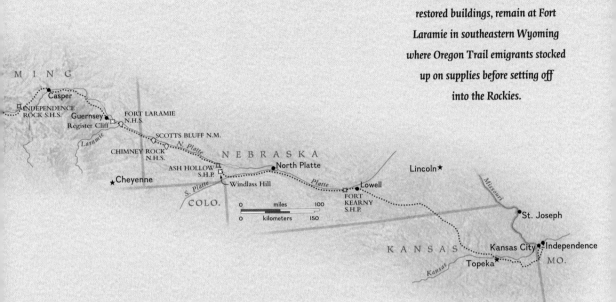

MING

Casper

INDEPENDENCE
ROCK S.H.S.

Guernsey
Register Cliff

FORT LARAMIE
N.H.S.

SCOTTS BLUFF N.M.

Laramie

N. Platte

CHIMNEY ROCK
N.H.S.

NEBRASKA

ASH HOLLOW
S.H.P.

North Platte

Lincoln ★

Windlass Hill

Platte

Lowell

★Cheyenne

S. Platte

COLO.

FORT
KEARNY
S.H.P.

Missouri

St. Joseph

0   miles   100

0   kilometers   150

KANSAS

Kansas City

Independence

Topeka

MO.

Kansas

Located in a secluded portion of Oregon's Columbia River Gorge, Elowah Falls drops 289 feet into a beautiful creek bed littered with moss-and-leaf-covered rocks. A hiking trail permits access to this spectacular site.

you've got an answer for the children—yes, we're there. We may not be at journey's end, but we're in the honest-to-god West.

It was only one third of the way to the Willamette Valley, but Ash Hollow was—and still is—the first real Western-looking place on the Oregon Trail. It also served as a microcosm of the trials and joys indicative of the entire trek: Here were shivarees and campfire sing-alongs, as well as wagon wrecks and cholera outbreaks. The worst killer on the trail, cholera was especially notorious at crowded water holes; a lone remaining grave marker—that of 18-year-old Rachel Pattison, who died in 1849—recalls the scores that died at Ash Hollow

from cholera. And yet another traveler remarked, "Nothing we have yet seen can exceed the beauty of Ash Hollow."

The Oregon Trail was like that—filled with births, adventures, weddings, deaths—all the experiences of life, packed into a six-month trip. It is the most famous of our historic trails for good reason: This trail and its cutoffs carried the most extensive migration in peacetime history, some 500,000 people moving more than 2,000 miles from 1841 to 1869. Most of these travelers actually ended up in California, Utah, or somewhere else besides Oregon, but for the 707 miles between Fort Kearny, Nebraska, and Fort Bridger, Wyoming, the route was the same.

Few people went to California in the early years, and with Francis Parkman's colorful 1848 book, *The Oregon Trail*, the name stuck.

Today the official trail covers 2,170 miles of Missouri, Kansas, Nebraska, Wyoming, Idaho, and Oregon—a little more than half of it on private land, 27 percent on federal land, and 20 percent on state land. Farms, highways, and developments have obscured about 85 percent of the trail, but the rest—more than 300 miles—is fairly well intact. There are still places, particularly in Wyoming, where miles of ruts and tracks carved by thousands of iron-rimmed wheels remain visible. Visitor centers, often located near major landmarks such as Ash Hollow, introduce the area's emigrant and natural history, and you can usually find a paved road closely paralleling the trail. But there are also lots of primitive road opportunities, sometimes directly on the Oregon Trail, beckoning true "rut nuts"; many landowners, especially those with open range, let you visit sites on their property as long as you ask for permission.

In 1841, you didn't need to ask anybody, except maybe your wife and children. That was the year 500 people started out

Wooden wagon wheels rest on the prairie in Bayard, Nebraska, where tours of the trail can be taken by covered wagon to places such as nearby Chimney Rock.

together from Independence. Unorganized, they had no guide and no clue about the route; most eventually turned back, although a few struggled on to California and about 30 made it to Oregon. Over the ensuing years many would begin with a common destination, then, after crossing the Continental Divide in western Wyoming, some would head to Oregon, others to California. Trail rumors could change minds overnight—farming was better in Oregon, or opportunities were wider in California. In any event, what had started as an exercise in navigation along old Indian and trapper routes grew to a veritable highway, complete with traffic jams at river crossings. By 1850 some 65,000 people used the trail. There was only about a 45-day window of time in late spring, just as the grass was greening and the mud was drying, when you could cross the mountains before the first snow. That means that in the 1850 season, an average of 1,500 people took to the trail daily—gaining 15 miles per day, there would have been 100 people per mile. At times the Oregon Trail was a village on wheels.

Why did so many travelers take the risk? A financial depression convinced many to

Pioneers listen attentively to stories of the hazards ahead in this 1853 painting, "Advice on the Prairie." One woman heard

that "Indians would kill us before we got to Oregon." She reported later that the native people were "better than represented."

sell their farms and try their luck out West. To missionaries, western Indians were fertile soil for sowing God's word. Some went for the adventure, with no intention of staying. And over this whole movement hovered the notion that it was America's Manifest Destiny to extend from the Atlantic to the Pacific. Britain and the United States hadn't agreed on an exact border for the Northwest in the early years of the trail. The flood of settlers linked the nation firmly with Oregon country, and in 1848 it became an official U.S. territory; the government's offer of free land to new settlers in the 1850s further accelerated booming populations.

People today follow the trail because it leads into the past. Mary Conway and her fiancé, Allen Statler, from Whitehall, Pennsylvania, recently spent 34 days on the Oregon Trail in their Itasca Suncruiser. They stopped at forts, museums, and landmarks all along the way, sometimes walking through tall-grass fields and crawling under barbed-wire fences. "I didn't go into a lot of detail whenever I taught history," says Mary, a retired kindergarten teacher. "We would talk about covered wagons and things like that, but my understanding of the westward movement has grown by leaps and bounds. It was a wonderful trip across our country." A friend in another motor home, Esther Rae Weinstein, did the navigating: "I had a CB microphone in one hand, a computer in the other, a spiral notebook in my lap, AAA maps, an emigrant trail book, brochures, and a GPS. Someone asked, 'Did you see

that sight?' and I said, 'Who has time to watch? I'm too busy!'"

The emigrants could not help seeing the sights. A large rock formation on the horizon might seem only a few miles off to Easterners unused to the West's wide-open spaces, yet it could take days to reach. Natural landmarks gave form to the trail and often took travelers' minds off the rigors of walking. The landmark that received the most attention in travelers' journals was Chimney Rock, a 300-foot-high spire of red clay and sandstone not far from today's Nebraska-Wyoming border. Reaching it meant the settlers were approaching the high plains and mountains.

Today this tower is a national historic site, still striking in its stark exclamation against the sky. To some pioneers it must have seemed a cenotaph, to others a beacon of hope. Far on the western horizon lie Scotts Bluff and other formations, while Chimney Rock makes a lone stand here, surrounded by nothing but sage and yucca and buffalo grass. Late afternoon shadows etch it into sharp relief. Gravel roads off Highway 92 take you to within a half mile; from there you can walk, though climbing on the rock is discouraged to prevent erosion.

You can also get there by covered wagon with an outfit called Oregon Trail Wagon Trains, which for the last 30 years has given modern travelers a taste of trail life. Wagon master Terry Murphy, or "Murph," has been here off and on since the beginning; he has appeared in documentaries and gun-fighting

A buffalo takes a break from grazing near South Pass, Wyoming. These animals once appeared as "solid masses as far as the eye could reach," according to one trail emigrant, who added happily, "we had fresh meat galore."

shows. At 46, he is a tall, thin slice of Western Americana. The wagons are authentic replicas, but horses do the pulling instead of oxen. The trail was once littered with dead and rotting oxen, discarded like worn-out engines. Bored children would use them for trampolines. "The oxen just got weak from pulling them wagons," Murph explains. "They walked for so many days. You do that and I guarantee you'll get weak. The pioneers had it rough—we don't know how soft this world has got."

The most important outpost on the trail, Fort Laramie in eastern Wyoming, was another sought-after landmark for emigrants. Here they could stock up on supplies, re-shoe their animals, make repairs, and get some much-

needed rest. During the trail's lifetime, the fort evolved from a small fur-trading post to a sprawling military complex, headquarters for the government's war against the Indians. Exhibits here focus on the Army, and a stroll through the grounds and reconstructed buildings gives you a feel for what travelers once experienced. The white frame Old Bedlam, the state's oldest standing building, was built in 1849 for bachelor officers; the beds covered with buffalo blankets and the card-strewn tables give the impression of an interrupted game. Down at the sibilant Laramie River, tributary to the Platte, you can see where emigrants hauled their wagons up. In early summer, fluff from cottonwoods blows across the stream, and the pulse of life quickens.

Red rock colors sage-covered Wyoming rangelands. Emigrants took in this vista just before entering South Pass, which

ascends to 7,550 feet. Due to the gentle incline, many pioneers did not realize they were crossing the Continental Divide.

Rifles at the ready, the 19th-century Cavalry Barracks at Fort Laramie, Wyoming, have been accurately restored. Established as a fur-trading post in 1834, the site was taken over by the military in 1849 to protect overland emigrants.

There's a sense of expectancy, of urgency, the wind reminding you not to linger—there are still mountains to cross.

Just to the west thousands of people did pause, at least briefly, to immortalize themselves at Register Cliff by carving their names into the rock wall. Though weathering and vandalism have taken a toll, many names and dates are still clearly visible. A fence now protects part of the wall, a compromise between authenticity and preservation. The surrounding area remains free of development, save for the dirt road in. Just as interesting as the names are the cliff swallows darting overhead, to and from their hundreds of gourd-shaped mud nests.

Three miles west lie the most outstanding ruts on the entire Oregon Trail. For much of the route, wagons used to spread out—sometimes 20 or more abreast—to avoid eating each other's dust. But some places offered only a single lane, creating bottlenecks such as one near the present town of Guernsey, where wagons had to trundle over the soft sandstone between the river and a hill. Over the years, ruts five feet deep were gouged into the rock. It's a popular site today, though there's no visitor center—just a small parking lot and footpath to the ruts. You can't help but be awed by what looks like an ancient Roman highway out in the middle of the American wilderness.

As the emigrants neared the Continental Divide about halfway along the trek and saw the snow-topped backbone of the Wind River Range, they had reason to thank the early fur trappers. Amid icy crags rearing up nearly 14,000 feet, those intrepid early explorers had found South Pass: at only 7,550 feet, it's so gentle and wide that many people went right through without realizing they had crossed the Divide.

Its gateway status makes South Pass one of the most significant landmarks of the trail. But what really sets off this area is its breathtaking beauty. For 125 miles, the trail passes through a gulf of high, wind-buffeted rangeland. From the highway, unbroken vistas reel out to buttes and mountains more than 30 miles away. A pair of all-but-deserted mining towns lie hidden in the brawny hills off Highway 28. Farther along, cowboys occasionally herd cattle across the road. Beyond is all sage and wildflowers clinging low to the range, while white clouds race across brilliant patches of blue. The trail cuts south of the highway, via a rough road. You'll need a sturdy vehicle,

Near Guernsey, Wyoming, five-foot-deep grooves carved in solid rock remain from the weight of thousands of wagons that proceeded here in a single file.

and—for the last mile—a good pair of boots. It's a lonely place, heralded only by a few markers and spectacular views. But you don't need to stand on the pass to appreciate the area—anywhere along the highway will do. You can even drive or walk along the actual trail, following twin tracks that slope westward toward the land of promise. It's not fenced off. In fact, traffic has helped maintain the trail by keeping vegetation down.

Preservation here is more a matter of protecting the view, something that the 4,000-member Oregon-California Trails Association (OCTA) feels strongly about. "Our biggest concern," says former OCTA president Dave Welch, "is development activities. We want places like South Pass to look as much as possible like what the pioneers saw. We're working now with the oil and gas industries, as well as private landowners to help them understand what they have. In a lot of cases the pioneers chose the best route, so it makes sense that people might want to put a pipeline or a fiber optic cable there, too." Welch and others are trying to preserve these areas.

After South Pass, the main route headed southwest to Fort Bridger, then turned northwest into Idaho. Some pioneers avoided this by taking risky shortcuts that could, with luck, shave days off the itinerary. Though Indian attacks were greatly feared, in actuality they ranked low on the risk scale. One traveler even wrote, "How I wish the Indians would attack—I'm so bored."

Six to 10 percent of the pioneers died on the way, often to disease or accidents—roughly ten per mile. Indians did kill several hundred people; Idaho in the 1850s was the most likely place and time. While Native Americans saw the first few wagon trains as curiosities, they considered succeeding hordes a threat—emigrants took game and forage, and spread disease and suspicion. Still, more Indians were killed by overlanders, and each major Indian attack was followed by a swift backlash from the U.S. Army.

Like any good tale, the western terrain delivered its climax at the end. After conquering the Blue Mountains of eastern Oregon and nearing their goal, the pioneers had the toughest part of their journey before them. Instead of the red carpet they deserved for the final 90 miles to Oregon City, they had a devil's choice to get around snowcapped Mount Hood. They could pay the Hudson's Bay Company $50 per wagon and $10 per person to go down the roiling Columbia River; many people also paid with their lives. Or, after 1846, they could pay $5 per wagon to cross Barlow Pass. Most chose the latter; it was both safer and cheaper. It was also a torment of rocks, roots, logs, and creeks. A forest of giant trees like nothing the pioneers had ever seen shut out the possibility of livestock forage. On several steep places wagons had to be lowered with ropes and drags. Imagine the complaints: "I paid a week's wages for this?"

Modern motorists who want to bump along the old Barlow Road in four-wheel-drive vehicles will be happy to know that the U.S. Forest Service maintains about 23 miles of it, just off Route 48. Or you can simply cruise through Barlow Pass on Highway 35; to the west, the Pioneer Woman's Grave commemorates an unknown emigrant whose trail ended just short of the Willamette Valley. From here, a one-mile hike takes you to the best ruts in the area—a trench five feet deep. Also here, just a few miles from a busy ski area, old-growth forests still stand.

Today, most travelers take the Columbia Gorge route, with its waterfalls and wild-flowered hiking trails. The southern way, via Highway 35 and US 26, is just as scenic; combining both routes makes for a fairly simple one-day loop—simpler than any of the 180 days the pioneers spent on the trail. Yet who wouldn't trade that day for a chance to go back in time, just for a while, to see what the land was like, and to feel the irresistible pull of the Oregon Trail? ◆

A western larch glows in an autumn Oregon scene.
The species is only one of two conifers that sheds its
needles in winter.

CHAPTER 7

CALIFORNIA TRAIL

Gray, half-frozen Donner Lake in California's Sierra Nevada offers a grim reminder of the tragedy
that befell the Donner Party of emigrants in the winter of 1846-1847. Trapped by early snow,
many starved to death; others resorted to cannibalism.

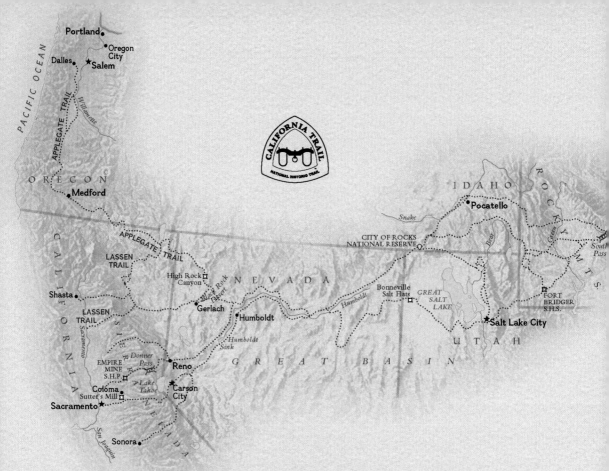

I wish California had sunk into the ocean before I had ever heard of it....
That desert has played hell with us.

—JAMES WILKINS, 1849

L et's get it out in the open: The California Trail was about greed. There is something distinctly, crazily American about mobs of people walking 2,000 torturous miles, of their own free will, for the remote chance of digging a fortune out of the ground. If the Oregon Trail was the hardworking farmer and the Mormon Trail the earnest pilgrim, the California was the get-rich-quick dreamer.

For the first 700 miles or so, these three trails were one and the same. They began at various jumping-off points along the Missouri River; traveled the Platte,

North Platte, and Sweetwater Rivers; and finally branched off from each other in southwestern Wyoming. The only difference was the destination. And the destination was governed by motive. Sure, prior to 1848 plenty of people went to California for the good climate and soil. But what really pounded the trail into dust were the wagons and boots of the gold seekers. From the discovery of gold at Sutter's Mill in 1848 through the 1850s, more than 200,000 people journeyed overland to California.

The 5,665 miles of the California Trail make it the longest of the national historic trails and reflect its many variations—no

WYOMING
Casper
INDEPENDENCE
ROCK S.H.S.
Register Cliff
FORT LARAMIE
N.H.S.
Torrington
SCOTTS BLUFF N.M.
CHIMNEY
ROCK N.H.S.
Cheyenne
COLO.
S. Platte
NEBRASKA
Loup
Omaha
Council Bluffs
IOWA
Lincoln
Nebraska City
Platte
Little Blue
MO.
St. Joseph
Kansas City
Independence
KANSAS
Topeka
Kansas
miles
100
kilometers
150

Below: After sawmill foreman James Marshall found tiny nuggets of gold in 1848 at Sutter's Mill (a working replica of which is seen in the distance), a mad stampede for California began.

Cattle graze on a hillside in Sonora, California, an area once aswarm with gold seekers. Of the conditions he endured, one miner wrote: "We all live more like brutes than humans."

less than 19 recognized cutoffs and alternate routes, all of them shortcuts to the goldfields. But, as the overlanders discovered, there was no easy way to easy street. Their El Dorado was waiting for them not at the end of a rainbow but across the hellish deserts of the Great Basin.

Getting over the Sierras before snowfall meant being in North America's largest desert at the worst possible time—in the scorching heat of August. Whether or not they saw any morality tale in their quest for gold, they kept on coming. The sheer quantity of journals written by one-time authors indicates that they certainly knew they were part of something bigger than them-

selves—they were swept up in a major historical movement. One emigrant wrote, "It will be received as a legend on the borderland of myth." Even though the gold rush did not peak until 1852, the momentum of foot traffic and settlement in 1850 helped hasten the statehood of California; only two years after being acquired from Mexico, it was admitted to the Union as the 31st state.

Nearly one-fifth of the trail's total mileage shows ruts or traces today, and more than 300 historic sites have been or are being developed for modern travelers—some are full-facility visitor centers, others little more than a lonely sign off a deserted road. Some 38 percent of the trail traverses public land, so while you can travel long unblemished sections you can't really do the entirety. Various groups stage annual reenactments of parts of the trail. Perhaps the most complete rerun in recent years was a 1999 wagon train from St. Joseph, Missouri, to Coloma, California, to celebrate the sesquicentennial of the 1849 gold rush.

Kay Threlkeld, interpretive planner for the California National Historic Trail, was a participant in that four-month trek. She laughs now about an invaluable experience that was "in many ways the worst summer of my life. You can read about alkali dust feet thick till the cows come home, but until you have been in a wagon on a hot summer afternoon when the dust is so thick that you can't breathe, you don't know."

She admits that compared to 1849, her trip was easy. Caterers fed them at night, and shuttles took them into town for showers. "I kept thinking," she says, "if I had to stay out here and gather up cow chips and make bread and take care of the kids, I'd just scream."

At any rate, re-creating a completely authentic expedition from 1850 is impossible; too much has changed. "Streams and creeks that flowed freely back then don't anymore," says Threlkeld. "But during the day when you're in the original springless wagons, or walking as many of us did, the experience hasn't changed much. There are some places along the trail where it's so pristine it's almost scary to look back and see wagons coming toward you because you know you're seeing exactly the same view that they saw 150 years ago."

The greatest hardship came from another aspect of the trail that has not changed—human nature. "The same problems of a small group of people in too close quarters for too long still exist today. And you begin to understand why, when those sorts of situations erupted in the 1850s, the parties split. I completely understood why the emigrants started shooting each other along the Humboldt River [in Nevada]. That's the point when you've just about had it."

The first part of the emigrants' journey took them across the length of Nebraska, from the tall-grass prairies to the plains. Then on they went to the broken-up lands of the high plains, counting off one landmark after another—Chimney Rock, Scotts Bluff, Fort Laramie, and Register Cliff. At Independence Rock in what is now central Wyoming, they stopped to carve their names or paint them in wagon tar. They were on schedule if they arrived around July 4, the day that members of an 1830 wagon train named this granite slab while celebrating the nation's birthday.

Modern travelers on Highway 220 are likewise drawn here; the rock rises from a sea of rangeland mottled with sagebrush, wildflowers, and grassy tufts. A casual trail about a mile long circles the rock, and you can even scale the rock itself, as did many of the more energetic pioneers. The view from

Workers in Nevada County mined more than half the gold found during the California gold rush.

Empire Mine, which operated from 1850 to 1956, contributed to the boom—it is now a state park.

136 feet up is only slightly better than from the ground in this wide open country, but such a natural pedestal has always beckoned the stout of heart. The pioneers would not have seen the seagulls and herons that now wing by on their way to nearby reservoirs created by damming the Medicine Bow and North Platte Rivers.

Nor would the pioneers have had the advantage of the little towns that dot the trail today. Livestock and agricultural towns include places like Torrington, Wyoming. It has 5,700 people, 24 churches, half a dozen bars, and a three-block Main Street. You can also find Saturday night bingo at the American Legion; the double-screen Wyoming Theatre; the Kelly Bean factory, the Ammo Shack with "Gun of the Week" specials; Wild Bill's Taxidermy; the friendly Broncho Bar that has stuffed the heads of nine deer, three moose, three bighorn, and an elk; and the incessant clatter of coal cars headed east during the day and returning empty at night.

At Independence Rock the pioneers followed the Sweetwater River west. They headed through the Rockies at gentle South Pass, which marked the halfway point of their trip. From here, the main route went southwest to Fort Bridger, where travelers

Restored 19th-century buildings from the trading post at Fort Bridger in southwest Wyoming include a butcher shop/warehouse, and a three-story log icehouse.

could stock up on depleted supplies. The fort began in 1843 as a private trading post run by mountain man and scout Jim Bridger and his partner Louis Vasquez. Ten years later the Mormons "obtained" it; whether by paying for it or by simply driving Bridger out because he was a perceived threat, the historical record is unclear. From 1858 until its abandonment in 1890, the fort served off and on as a U.S. military outpost.

Today it lies just off the interstate at the edge of Fort Bridger town. Although the fort still has many buildings from its army days, the most interesting thing here is a reconstructed trading post. With its stockade fence, crude log frame, and dirt floor, it presents a telling image of the Jim Bridger period in history. Run as a gift shop, it displays the kinds of wares that would have been for sale in the 1840s—European knives and pistols, Indian blankets, powder horns, wooden games, lanterns, bonnets, materials to make Mexican jewelry, Canadian coonskin caps, and bull scrotum pouches. Costumed mountain men and women are sometimes on hand to demonstrate tomahawk throwing.

One mountain woman, 49-year-old Debbie Devish, cuts a striking figure in her

The Bonneville Salt Flats stretch in a seemingly endless expanse of salt and alkali deposits. Formed when the ancient Lake Bonneville disappeared about 15,000 B.C., the flats rest at an altitude of 4,000-plus feet. Overland travelers found this place terrifying; but since 1900, automobile enthusiasts have raced cars across its hard, flat surface, setting a number of speed and endurance records.

long blue skirt, black boots, leggings, and an elk-tooth necklace—made from an animal she shot. She often works in the gift shop, though she is an ace with her homemade tomahawk: "If I get to thinking too hard I come out here and throw my 'hawk to relax."

From Fort Bridger, California-bound pioneers jogged northwest to the Snake River Basin in Idaho, then southwest into the jumbled terrain called City of Rocks— others continued on to Oregon. In 1850 emigrant John Steel described the City of Rocks: "Here were pyramids of white granite that rival the world-renowned wonders of the Nile; rocks in the form of castles with

domes and turrets, spires rising probably 500 feet, and nicely balanced on the point of some of them large pieces of granite."

Entering present-day Nevada, the trail dropped down to the curving Humboldt River, the pioneers' lifeline in the desert. But what a lifeline! Here was a river that grew smaller as it went downstream, finally disappearing altogether in the Humboldt Sink. Its water often was a thin gruel of warm brackish mud. Local springs were either scalding hot or so alkaline they were poisonous. What little grass grew along the trail that wasn't dried by the summer sun was sheathed in salt crystals. An

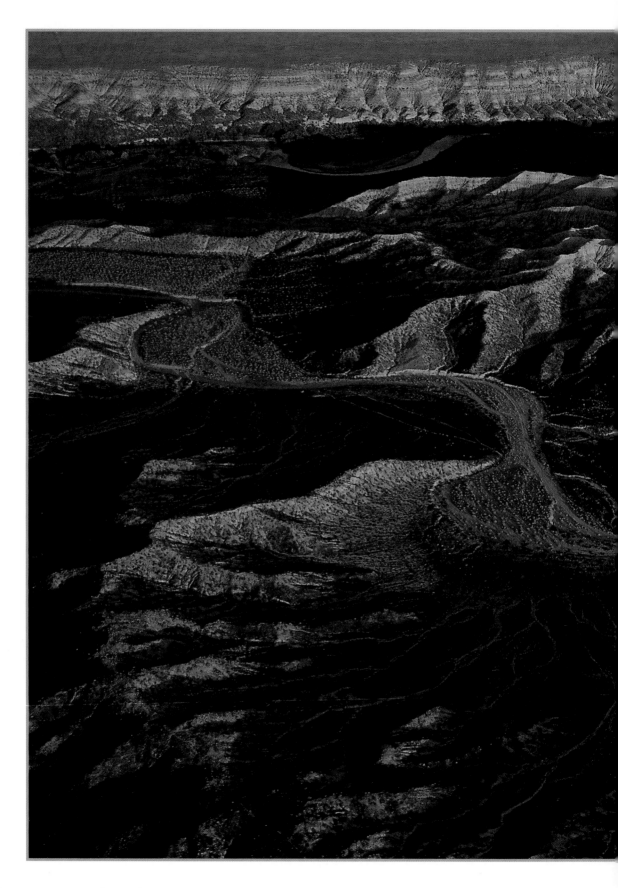

A source of misery for westering pioneers, the Humboldt River—named for German scientist Baron von Humboldt—was

often referred to contemptuously as "the Humbug" because it snakes across Nevada then peters out in the Nevada sands.

A wary, and well-armed, prospector heads to a new mining camp. To stake a claim during the California gold rush a miner had only to leave his tools at the site—but a rifle might help settle disputes.

emigrant wrote, "There is not a fish nor any other living thing to be found in its waters, and there is not timber enough in three hundred miles of its desolate valley to make a snuff-box."

The pioneers were now in the Great Basin, that vast and forbidding high-elevation land of salt flats and dead-end streams between the Rockies and the Sierra Nevada. An 1849 traveler described it as "one of the most detestable countries God ever made, to say nothing of its sterility and barrenness." At night it was so cold water would freeze; during the day

the sun would bake the ground. A powder-fine dust, kicked up by the animals and wagon wheels, coated every crevice of clothing and skin. Paiute and Washoe Indians, driven to starvation by the loss of game along the trail, harassed the wagon trains like hornets, stealing oxen for food in the middle of the night.

As for the animals themselves, the California Trail proved grim indeed. A team of two to six oxen or mules might go all day across the desert, dragging the equivalent of a modern car 20 miles without food or water, their necks bloody against the yoke.

Refusal earned them the cutting end of a bullwhacker's whip. In some instances, desperate for water, they would stampede into the wasteland where they would die. Other times they simply dropped dead in their harnesses. A few diarists sounded a note of pity, writing, for example, of the joy the oxen took standing in water to their knees at the end of a hard day. One writer counted 163 dead oxen, mules, and horses in a 16-mile stretch. The trail relic you're most likely to find today, at least in the desert, is a bleached bone.

The trail across Nevada is among the most visually stunning of any of the historic trails. Interstate 80 follows the Humboldt River, but you need to get off that high-speed freeway to appreciate the surrounding terrain. Near the town of Humboldt, one branch to California called the Applegate-Lassen Route heads off into the Black Rock Desert, a harshly beautiful empire of salt and dust and silence. Seasonally dry lake beds called playas crack into scaly patterns; dust devils bloom miles

A sign near Alder Creek in California's Tahoe National Forest alerts hikers that they are on part of the historic route taken by the ill-fated Donner party.

away across snow-white alkali flats; shimmering hillsides are mirages of ruined stonework.

Up in the remote fastness of High Rock Canyon, basalt sculptures stand out against a crystalline sky. The occasional greasewood shrub and iodine bush are tenacious miracles amid the dry land. "I'll give you a warning," says author and guide Chuck Dodd. "Don't go out in the Black Rock Desert alone. People get lost. People occasionally get dead out there."

But for those who cannot resist, one of Black Rock's main entry points is the dusty town of Gerlach, population 150, positioned at what appears to be the end of the Earth. Sitting on a branch of the California Trail, this 1905 railroad town boasts four bars and one gas station; beside a shack rises a 15-foot-high tree of cow skulls and ribs. The blacktop does continue north, but it's 82 miles to the next town. Dirt roads and tracks snake out over the desert to ghost towns and pioneer water holes. Wise travelers off on a day jaunt take camping gear and enough food and water for several days; if the playa is at all wet—and it can be hard to tell until you're in the middle of one—vehicles are likely to get stuck and help could be far, far away.

The trail's final pitch, over the Sierra Nevada, was the ultimate test in a five-month ordeal—for some, it proved too much. The Donner party of 1846 was already the last wagon train of the season. Taking advice from a letter written by a man no one had even heard of, they wasted precious weeks hacking a road through the mountains of Utah in a vain attempt to save time, livestock, and their possessions. Exhausted, the group, which contained people mostly under the age of 20, disintegrated into a bickering, leaderless bunch of families. Then winter came early to the Sierras that year, penning the Donners down on the east side of the mountains in late October. Snowdrifts up to 20 feet deep plagued the party—the sort of drifts that would not be seen in the area again for 100 years. Timing was everything.

"Never take no cutoffs, and hurry along as fast as you can," wrote 13-year-old Donner party member Virginia Reed in a letter. What she saw and endured defies description. Of the 91 people that started together, 42 succumbed to starvation and exposure, their bodies becoming life-sustaining food for the survivors.

Nestled in a forest of lodgepole pine and white fir below what is now Donner Pass, Donner Memorial State Park today preserves a part of the group's winter camp-site. From the museum, you can wander down through a grove of towering, bird-filled evergreens to a boulder that formed the wall and fireplace of one cabin, and you can boat on Donner Lake, a pleasant, wind-ruffled body of water. Farther removed from the noise of the interstate, the more evocative Alder Creek site lies a few miles north in a willowy wetland flecked with sunflowers and purple penstemons. It was here that Tamsen Donner stayed with her dying husband, refusing to leave with the rescue parties. When they returned in the spring, she was dead.

"Westward ho! Who wants to go to California without costing them anything?" began the ad placed by George Donner for ox-team drivers. The cost though, he found, could be everything.

Yet if the Donner saga of 1846 was a cautionary story, it was not enough to stop the legions from coming. All were aiming for the Sierra's western foothills, the land of golden dreams. Most did not expect to stay. But when they discovered that the true riches of the Sacramento Valley were to be found in planting instead of panning, they put down roots. The farmers, ranchers, and merchants were the ones who struck pay dirt, and on their shoulders the golden state was built. ◆

Fantastic rock formations dazzle visitors to the City of Rocks National Reserve in southernmost Idaho. Some of the ancient rocks date back to 2.5 billion years ago.

CHAPTER 8

MORMON PIONEER TRAIL

As dawn breaks over the horizon, Chimney Rock in western Nebraska appears as a majestic spire against the colorful sky. Dramatically rising 450 feet above the North Platte River, it was declared "awfully sublime" by one overland traveler.

Come, come ye Saints, no toil nor labor fear,

But with joy wend your way;

Tho' hard to you this journey may appear.

—Hymn penned by
William Clayton, 1846

"Hard" barely begins to describe the tragedy and suffering endured by many on the Mormon Pioneer Trail, which claimed nearly 6,000 lives. Yet the 1846 hymn, penned near the beginning of the Mormon exodus to Utah, captures the spirit of almost cheerful stoicism inspired by the trail. The more the tribulation, the greater the glory. Not man's glory of course, but God's.

Of the many religious movements to spring up in 19th-century America, none was more successful than the Church of Jesus Christ of Latter-Day Saints (LDS). And no era is more important to Mormon history than the trail of 1846-1869. For latecomers, the completion of the transcontinental railroad in 1869 made the way easier. But for early Mormons the trail was a rite of passage, for their descendants a badge of honor; it was likened to the exodus of the Israelites from Egypt. Declared a national historic trail in 1978, the Mormon Pioneer Trail was among the first four designated.

But why, some may wonder, does it deserve separate billing? After all, the trail was not even blazed by Mormons. Most of it traverses the same route as the Oregon and California Trails, which a half million emigrants followed west; only 70,000 or so of that total were Mormon.

"I think it's not an issue of numbers," says Salt Lake City Mormon Church historian Michael Landon. "It's an issue of purpose. There was more social cohesion. They were refugees starting a whole new lifestyle and culture. This unique purpose of the trail is why it merits recognition."

Indeed, the Mormon Trail was unique in several respects. For one thing, Mormons traveled mostly on the north side of the

Elkhorn

Missouri

West Nishnabotna

Des Moines ★

0 · miles · 100
0 · kilometers · 150

N E B R A S K A

Loup

Omaha

Council Bluffs

I O W A

Des Moines

Platte

Grand Island

Lincoln ★

Mount Pisgah

North Platte

Nauvoo

ILL.

M I S S O U R I

Mississippi

An aerial view reveals Nebraska's Platte River, once a trail marker for Mormon pioneers.

Platte River, opposite the Oregon Trail, partly because they had started there and partly to keep themselves separate (to avoid hate mongers, as much as anything else).

Of all the people heading west in the mid-1800s, the Mormons were the most organized. Instead of a few families at a time, hurrying toward the promise of land or gold, the Mormons were really one large group fleeing persecution and heading toward a new utopia.

And since they were going together or not at all, theirs was a two-way road. While most of the non-Mormons on the other side of the Platte were too hell-bent-for-Oregon to cast a backward glance, the Mormons were constantly going back and forth—helping those still struggling on the trail, smoothing out the rougher spots, and sending missionaries East for more souls. As Pulitzer prize-winning novelist (and non-Mormon) Wallace Stegner writes in his still definitive 1964 book *The Gathering of Zion: The Story of the Mormon Trail*, "By the improvements they made in it, they earned the right to put their

A fungi-covered tree trunk lies in a forest west of Nauvoo, Illinois. The Mormons left Nauvoo and marched 1,300 miles to the valleys of the Great Salt Lake.

name on the trail they used." Today about 36 percent of this trail traverses public lands, most prominently in Wyoming where long stretches can be explored by foot or four wheel drive. The rest is closely paralleled by an easy-to-follow driving route that courses through some of the West's most spectacular scenery.

The Mormon Pioneer Trail begins in Nauvoo, Illinois, a sleepy hamlet on the Mississippi River. Just about a thousand people inhabit this pleasant little town today known as much for its blue cheese as its connection with the Mormons. In summer, a scattering of tourists stroll its wide, shady streets, peek into its historic homes, catch dinner at the unpretentious old Hotel Nauvoo, and take in a musical about the early town.

The deep pockets of the LDS account for what little tourism there is. History comes with the Mormon point of view, in a very low-key manner, without the kitsch of many other such reconstructions. Recent plans for rebuilding the original temple—torched after the Mormons left in 1846—have generated a new tension,

Mormon teamsters who guided Church-sponsored wagon trains carrying emigrants and supplies pose in 1866. Noted for their skill in traversing rough terrain, the so-called "Mountain Boys went along full of boldness & without accident."

some locals fearing over-development of their quiet village.

In late 1846, Nauvoo was the embattled center of Mormonism, its 12,000 resident believers making plans to evacuate and head west. Mormon founder Joseph Smith had been assassinated by an angry mob two years earlier, and hundreds of Mormon homes had been burned. An expanding church-state of industrious zealots, led by polygamous leaders who organized their own militia, was more than the provincial town could bear. Threats and violence raged, the Mormons often giving as good as they got. But enough was enough. It was time for the Mormons to pack up and go.

Mormonism might have become a historical footnote if not for the blue-chip management style of Brigham Young. Whereas Smith had been the charismatic visionary, Young became the suit. He was the corporate muscle that would motivate an estimated 70,000 willing, but untested, followers and get them across the Great Plains and the Rockies to the fertile valleys of the Great Salt Lake. He had already emerged as the leader among the bickering junta that followed Smith's death. So in February of 1847, the faithful hitched their wagons, and with a creak of iron-rimmed wheels went forth to their promised land. The Mississippi was their Red Sea and the fact that it was frozen,

A mother grieves over her child's grave as the stunned father looks out over the Mormon encampment on the Missouri

River known as Winter Quarters. Hundreds of emigrants died and were buried at this site in present-day Omaha.

In a modern-day reenactment, a driver helps children down from a covered wagon. On the trail accidents were common. Children often fell out of wagons or got lost amid the huge assemblage of wagons and families.

allowing easy passage, was taken as a sign of their deliverance despite the bitterness of winter.

Across Iowa in companies of tens, fifties, and hundreds they marched. Through bluestem prairies and oak forests, across icy streams and axle-sucking swamps they trudged onward. Listen to their proud lamentation—mud, wet food, irritable children, more mud, lost cattle, collapsing tents, sickness, death, and still more mud. They knew the Lord was testing them, and they bent their backs to the burden. There were some good days, too, when the Mormon band would play to a farm-town audience or boys would go out hunting. These were blessings to hoard, for the real

tribulations lay beyond the Mississippi—and even the plains. Stopping along the way to set up base camps, these green pioneers took 100 days to complete the 265 miles to their winter quarters, on the north side of present-day Omaha.

Today, trail sites are spotty on this first leg of the journey—markers in small towns and on the edges of cornfields make for a rough, connect-the-dots passage. But at Winter Quarters the Mormons were not content to set up temporary shelter. Even though their advance party, led by Brigham Young, would roll out for Utah in the spring, this would remain a staging area for a steady stream of pioneers. Almost overnight, 538 log cabins and 83 sod houses sprang up along with mills and a brickyard. Though little remains today of this village that once held more than 4,000 people, the Mormon Trail Center gives visitors a feel for what was here. You can tour on your own, but cheerful guides who call themselves Sister or Elder so-and-so and refer often to "our people" prefer to walk you around. They may press *The Book of Mormon* upon you as they give you their insights into trail history. The replica sod-roof house and wagon were made to exact specifications, and the reconstructed hand-cart here was actually used in the 1996-97 reenactment in which thousands participated, celebrating the trail's sesquicentennial. The cemetery across the street holds 365 pioneer graves and a life-size memorial that movingly reminds us of the Mormons' ordeal. Created in 1936 by sculptor Avard Fairbanks, the work depicts a couple, wrapped in windblown garments, huddling over the shallow grave of their child.

The second leg of the journey would take the pioneers almost to the Great Salt Lake—1,032 miles in 111 days. Instead of forging on together, a whole city on the move, the Mormons migrated a few "companies" at a time, armed with a prodigious amount of research. They interviewed explorers, studied maps and documents, and formulated a plan that included following some existing trails as well as gathering information en route. The Mormons would become the most dedicated of scribes on an emigration trail that inspired thousands of diaries and letters. With a Deuteronomic attention to detail, the Saints recorded their hegira: Brigham Young's group, for example, was composed of 143 men, 3 women, 2 boys, 72 wagons, 93 horses, 66 oxen, 52 mules, 19 cows, 17 dogs, and several chickens. They set up way stations to help later companies, invented an odometer to click off precise distances from one landmark to another, and after only a year they published a guidebook with the impressive title, *The Latter-Day Saints' Emigrants' Guide: Being a Table of Distances, showing all the springs, creeks, rivers, hills, mountains, camping places, and all other notable places from Council Bluffs to the Valley of the Great Salt Lake.* For Mormons and non-Mormons alike, it proved to be one of the most useful and comforting books on the long trail.

As the travelers rolled out across the open wind-swept plains of Nebraska and Wyoming, they followed the Platte, then the North Platte. Like other pioneers, the Mormons walked most of the way, covering more than 1,000 miles, while their animals carried the supplies. Miraculous beauty was evident everywhere, and it still is—especially beyond the confluence of the North and South Platte Rivers. Fierce thunderstorms would crack open the vault of sky, wind and rain rattling the ribs of the wagons and soaking the pioneers; then rainbows would arc across the limitless miles of grassland, and at night the stars would crowd the heavens like thousands of

Cliffs rising above the Green River in southwest Wyoming bear witness to the tenacity,

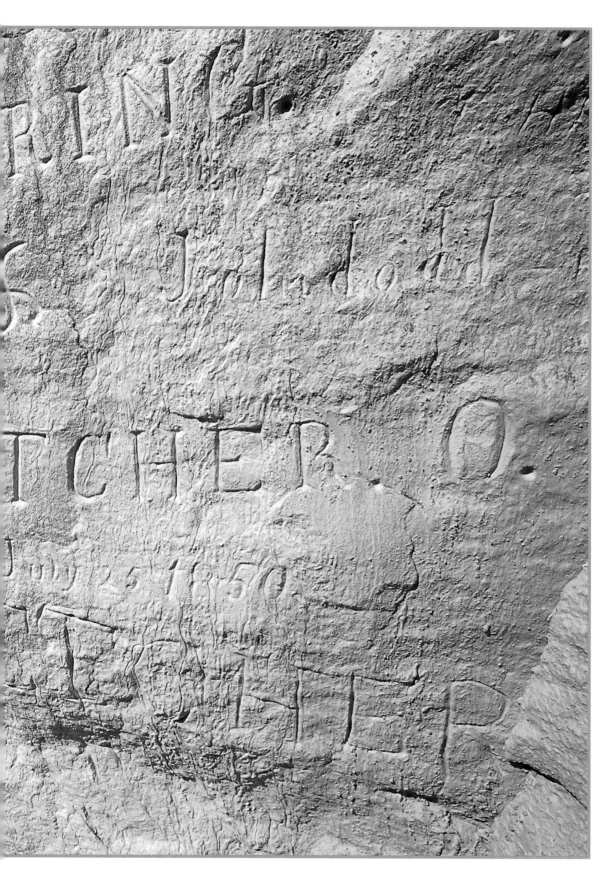

and survival, of overland travelers who carved their names in the soft limestone.

brilliant eyes. Today, travelers can zip across the same landscape in a few days instead of three months, the modern transportation making it all but impossible to conceive of being out in the open for so long.

A cold, sleety day may be the best time for experiencing the trail where it quits the North Platte and picks up with the Sweetwater River, just west of Casper, Wyoming. It was along here, at Martin's Cove, that the pioneer group called the Martin Handcart Company of 1856 met disaster. For many emigrants, the seven-foot-long handcarts were a cheap alternative to animal-drawn wagons. But production delays caused the handcart companies of 1856 to get a late start; still, they decided to push on anyway. The unseasoned wood of the hastily made carts soon began to shrink in the blazing sun. These were new pioneers, fresh from England —they didn't know that greasing their axles would cause windblown sand to stick to the grease and grind up the axles. Carts quickly became useless and were abandoned; loads were combined. The heavier-than-ever carts wore down

A rotting carcass fouls the air beyond South Pass where Mormons crossed the Rockies en route west. Brigham Young promised his faithful: "The angels of God will go with you."

men unaccustomed to such labors. Buffalo robes and warm blankets were tossed to lighten the loads—and then, in October, an early blizzard struck. Starving and exposed, the emigrants began to die. Old people dropped with fatigue; others died in their sleep. Survivors wasted precious strength burying the dead, then pressed on.

Finally, they moved up a ravine in the Granite Mountains and hunkered down in a camp west of Devil's Gate rock formation. There, they were unable to move for four days and were reduced to living on water, rawhide, and bark. Without the arrival of rescuers from Salt Lake City, all 576 men, women, and children would have perished. As it was, one quarter of them died; others lost hands and feet to frostbite, altogether making for the most tragic episode in the Mormon Trail's history.

In this now peaceful site along the Sweetwater known as Martin's Cove, the Mormon Handcart Visitor Center pulls no punches in describing the losses of 1856. A realistic film capturing the tragedy shows

Hauling their possessions—and small children—in two-wheeled wooden handcarts, Mormon families ford a prairie stream. "Let them come on foot with handcarts or wheelbarrows," leader Brigham Young once declared.

continuously, the narration drawn from a survivor's letter. But says Sister Mair, one of the many guides here: "We don't focus on the tragedy, but on what we can learn from them because of what they were willing to suffer. They were able to do a great many things because of their beliefs. It's amazing they didn't all die. You can call it faith, you can call it testimony, you can call it belief."

For most Mormon pioneers, Martin's Cove was just another landmark with a view to the next, the "gun sight" of Split Rock some 15 miles west. From here they continued along the Sweetwater with its reli-

able water and forage, leaving ruts still visible today. One woman recorded, "We have forever taken leave of the waters running toward the home of our childhood and youth...."

Then, they traveled over the Rockies at South Pass and on down to the swift, deep Green River, where the Lombard Ferry in southwestern Wyoming became one of the Mormons' early commercial enterprises. After weeks of buffalo-chip campfires and unforgiving sun, here they finally found trees. Unfortunately, wagon-train traffic could back up for days waiting to cross the more than 300-foot-wide river. Today this serene but little-visited spot sits at the edge of a wildlife refuge brimming with geese, ducks, and herons. The state highway passes through an open range where cattle, deer, and pronghorns graze unfenced; clever road signs warn motorists to stay alert—one has a moose silhouette and the words, "Heavy Traffic Ahead."

The final part of the journey, through the maze of the Wasatch Mountains, was the toughest part for the Mormons who followed and improved upon the trail blazed by the ill-fated Donner-Reed party of 1846. Today this section is one of the loveliest and most interesting ways to approach Salt Lake City. Interstate 80 threads through Echo Canyon, a 28-mile-long slot with striated walls and sculptural formations. The trail then yanks northwest to the town of Henefer where it picks up Highway 65 and ascends Hogsback Summit. The pioneers called it Heartbreak Ridge because they could get a view of the tall peaks still ahead that they had to cross. It's incredible how quiet this area is today, only 30 miles outside Salt Lake City; sheep graze the lonely sage-covered hills beside historical markers, and traffic is all but nonexistent.

Off a dirt road in nearby East Canyon, a hiking trail offers a chance to walk for several miles in the pioneers' footsteps. Unencumbered by wagons and handcarts, you can hardly feel the emigrants' pain; this walk up a willow-lined rocky streambed is pure delight today. Spruce and wind-whispered aspens freckle the path with shadows, while sunflowers brighten the meadows and deer watch from the woods. Atop Big Mountain you catch a glimpse of the pioneers' valley, but what steals the scene are the green-mantled hills leading to a triumphant blast of jagged, snowy peaks.

A zigzag road descends the other side of Big Mountain; here the Mormons had to lock their wagon wheels and drag logs behind to prevent runaways. Created in the 1990s for flood control and water supply, Little Dell Reservoir has drowned several miles of the trail. But Emigration Canyon Road roughly follows the route as it twists and turns down Little Mountain and through steep-walled Emigration Canyon. Then it opens up to an area where you can behold the city spreading out in the distance and recall Brigham Young's immortal words, "This is the place."

Today, at this location, a towering memorial to Young and other Mormon leaders anchors a historical park. Thousands of pioneers sought this same view, enduring months of challenging terrain and ordeals. Ahead lay years of more labors, as they worked to fulfill prophecy and make the desert "blossom as the rose." After 1,300 long miles, that was a mission they were eager to take on. ◆

Seagulls convene on the Great Salt Lake. In 1848, gulls helped Mormon settlers by eating a swarm of crickets that was devastating the crops.

CHAPTER 9

PONY EXPRESS TRAIL

Wild horses draw blood on the Wyoming rangelands. Amid the wild herds that still exist in the West are descendants of Pony Express steeds that were stolen by Native Americans.

...a man and a horse burst past our excited faces, and go winging away
like a belated fragment of a storm!

—MARK TWAIN, 1872

Like a flash of lightning, the red-shirted rider tears across the moonlit plain. He can't see it yet, but somewhere out in that vast sage-covered wilderness lies the station. A thunderhead builds from the west, and it begins to rain—softly at first, then in blinding sheets, the wind lashing the horse and rider. But they both know the way—even in the dark they can sense it in the lay of the land, the shifting of the darkened hills, the approaching coolness of a spring. Then they're upon it, a scattering of low stone buildings. A new rider emerges—within minutes, the mail pouch is with a fresh horse and whisked away.

From April 1860 to October 1861 the Pony Express carried mail between St. Joseph, Missouri, and Sacramento, California, faster than overland routes had ever moved before—

2,000 miles in 10 days. The fact that it actually worked made it a legend, and though the trail barely made a dent across the great American plains and deserts, the Pony Express has endured in the national scrapbook as a beloved symbol of never-say-die gallantry.

Today the national historic trail, designated in 1992, travels mostly across public lands, including a long and gloriously lonely stretch of 381 miles in Nevada. While the eastern third of the corridor has been altered by agricultural development, the rest is largely unspoiled rangeland. About 50 of the 190 stations still remain, many in ruins that evoke the passage of time.

With the mail traveling in two directions, the Pony began in both St. Joseph and Sacramento. Today the slight bias toward a westward journey is that it mimics the

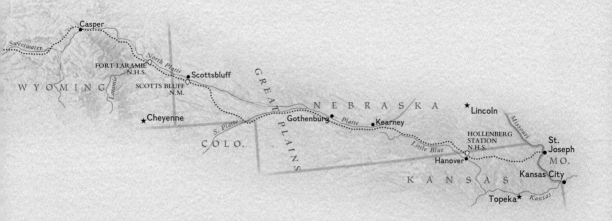

Utah's Wasatch Range proved a formidable—but not impossible—barrier for the legendary Pony Express riders.

Barbed wire littered with tumbleweed frames an expanse of Wyoming flatland. Pony Express riders raced across these lonely, open stretches despite the storms that often raged.

historic flow of the country, though you could logically follow the trail in either direction. Those who do begin in St. Joseph (locally known as St. Joe) generally start at the site of the original stables, now the Pony Express National Memorial. A museum that lays out the whole story, the memorial has enough push buttons to keep you entertained and enough text to make you feel informed. You can pump water from the original well, watch and hear an interactive diorama showing the trail's diverse terrain, and change a *mochila*—the leather flap that held the mail—from one saddle to another.

Two blocks up the street, the Patee House, now a museum, was a luxury hotel in 1860 and the headquarters for the Pony Express. Mail from the East would arrive at the train depot, the western terminus of the Hannibal and St. Joseph line. It was then transferred to the Pony office here. A rider would head out from St. Joseph to the Missouri River, which flanks the western end of town, take a ferry across, and begin relaying the mail forward.

Here is how it worked: Once a week, and later twice a week, mail would be sent from both ends of the Pony Express route. A rider would travel from 10 to 15 miles to a station, where he would pick up a fresh horse. Every 75 to 100 miles, he would come to a home station, where a new rider would take over. So each rider stayed in his home territory, going back and forth once or twice each week. The only thing that went the entire distance was the precious mochila. Recruitment posters advertised for "young, skinny, wiry fellows not over 18. Must be expert riders, willing to risk death daily. Orphans preferred." Though we can read in these ads the same kind of blustering pitch that appeals to extreme-sports enthusiasts, they weren't kidding, and few riders were older than 18.

The mail traveled 24 hours a day, almost always arriving on time. It shot out across the Kansas prairie, then up to the Platte River, where it followed the emigrant trail. The horses could keep a ten-mile-per-hour pace by carrying no more than 180 pounds: a 135-pound rider, 20 pounds of mail, and up to 25 pounds of equipment that included a saddle and revolver.

On the eastern part of the trail, ranch buildings often served as stations. For example, the Hollenburg Station, near the small town of Hanover, Kansas, was built in 1857 on a ranch beside the Oregon Trail. The owner sold food and supplies to overlanders, and later provided space for a

His hair neatly combed, young Thomas Owen King, Pony Express rider, calmly poses for the camera. On the trail, he once briefly lost his way in stirrup-high snow.

Pony Express station. Now a state historic site, the wood-frame structure holds exhibits on the emigrant trails and the Pony Express. Likewise, the Machette Station in Gothenburg, Nebraska, was a trading post and ranch house. Originally located about 15 miles west, the red-cedar station was moved in 1931 to a park in Gothenburg where it sits on prominent display and operates as a museum and gift shop. Probably it originally had a sod roof, but the wood building maintains the rustic flavor of the early stations.

By the time the mail reached Scotts Bluff, in western Nebraska, the prairie was giving way to the plains and riders were following the same trail as the emigrants who were bound for points west. Express riders were not always lone horsemen dashing across the wilderness; in many places, during the day, they might pass dozens of wagon trains and stagecoaches. Cheers would go up from the slow lane, to which the rider would give a quick wave as he bolted by, like a wind from the speed-loving future.

An 800-foot-high promontory of clay and sandstone, Scotts Bluff was one of the

Native American leaders gather for a peace conference at Fort Laramie in 1868. A way station on the Pony Express

route, the fort was also a crossroads for both white travelers and Indians who would come regularly to trade.

most famous landmarks on the Pony Express, Oregon, California, and Mormon Trails. Few Express riders stopped here on their way past, but emigrants often camped by the springs, their wagon ruts still clearly evident. Some scrambled to the top of the striated bluff for magnificent scenery—the whole continent, it would seem, spreading west. Modern visitors can walk or drive up for a similar view. The town of Scottsbluff now spreads to the east, and the persistent odor of cow manure reminds you that this country has long been tamed. Buffalo are out of the picture, but hawks still kite in the racing winds and there remains a grandeur in the largeness of the land.

After Nebraska, the trail carves the length of Wyoming, then down to Salt Lake City, following already established trails. But from this point the Pony makes an audacious sprint straight across the arid deserts of Utah and Nevada. You have to see this part of the trail to fully appreciate what a brash enterprise the whole thing was. Since there were few ranches out here, stations had to be built all the way across the desert. In what must rank as one of the country's most remarkable feats of privately funded logistics, the freighting and stagecoach firm of Russell, Majors, and Waddell put the Pony Express together in a mere two months. Without the use of a transcontinental telegraph, the firm had to hire 80 riders and 400 station attendants, buy 500 horses and have them delivered to the proper stations, organize freight wagons to go out,

and construct stations in some of the most dangerous countryside known. They also arranged for regular deliveries of food and water to the men and horses, set up offices on either end of the route, and advertised the new express mail service to the general public. To protect this tenuous system, the firm made its employees take an oath swearing "before the Great and Living God" that while working for the firm they would refrain from drinking and fighting, and would direct all their actions "to win the confidence" of their employers.

Never intended as a long-term solution to the problem of slow, cross-country mail, the Pony was more of a bold publicity stunt. Russell, Majors, and Waddell hoped to prove the advantage of a central mail route over the existing southern ones and thus gain a government mail contract. Subsidies would flow into company coffers like manna, and the company would then control the mail whether it eventually went by stage, railroad, or whatever. But it didn't happen that way.

Yes, the Pony was much faster than the southern stage route—more than twice as fast. Yet no government money followed. From the beginning, the operation was in financial trouble; often the firm had to dig deep into nearly empty pockets. A Paiute Indian uprising occurred only a month after the Pony began. Stations were attacked and burned all over Nevada, costing the lives of dozens of attendants and one rider. The service ground to a halt for a couple of months until peace was restored. During the

Two present-day employees of the Oregon Trail Wagon Trains in Nebraska chew the fat wagonside. Pony Express riders blazed past slower-moving wagon trains and stagecoaches—earning cheers as they passed.

same summer, William Russell embezzled bonds to keep the company from going under. Employees were now swearing a different kind of oath, referring to the Central Overland California & Pike's Peak Express Company (the Pony's official name) as the Clean Out of Cash & Poor Pay Express Company. The bond scandal made headlines, yet somehow the Pony continued in operation for another year.

One of the best preserved stations is about a 30-minute walk from US 50 in central Nevada. Though much of the route in Nevada lies far from the blacktop, or from any road of any kind, it crosses this deserted highway near Cold Springs Station. The roadside sign only indicates a "historical marker," then an information panel at the pulloff mentions the trail leading to the station. The lack of advertising helps preserve this pristine site from overuse. Enveloped by miles of rugged sage country, the basalt-rock station blends so well into its environment that you can't see it until you're a few hundred yards away. The only signs of midday life are buzzing insects amid the desiccated sage and the occasional jet streak overhead, though the region does hold herds of wild horses, some of them descended from Pony Express horses stolen by Indians. The station, a warren of small rooms, looks like something put together by Paleo-Indians thousands of years ago. It's hard to believe that anybody, no matter how much

Morning sun breaks through clouds near Kearney, Nebraska. Intrepid Pony Expressmen like 15-year-old William Cody would

race across western landscapes to deliver the mail. The boy later went on to international fame as "Buffalo Bill" Cody.

they loved solitude, could have lived out here. Explorer Richard Burton came through in 1860 and described it as "a wretched place, half built and wholly unroofed."

Dale Ryan, president of the National Pony Express Association (NPEA), believes these desert stations were not always without a roof. "I think they probably had some canvas on top. I don't see how they could survive out there in the summer without some kind of shade. And in winter the wind would've been unbearable." The NPEA helps maintain public awareness of the trail by sponsoring an annual re-ride of the entire route, a relay involving more than 500 riders.

In many ways, Nevada remains the toughest part of the trail. This is basin and range country. A flat land with heart-pounding blips, the terrain is composed of arid basins some 20 miles across, separated by thinly forested ranges that rise about 2,000 feet higher than the basins. Ryan himself once had to ride 35 miles—ten times the average distance—rather than risk a horse trailer getting stuck in a playa, an evaporation lake that can conceal a layer of mud.

The longest ride of the Pony Express was made in Nevada by Bob Haslam during the Paiute uprising. When his relief rider refused to pass into besieged territory, Haslam agreed to work a double shift. Then, after that heroic ride, with the mail from the East just in, he mounted up for the entire ride back, more than 320 miles through the meanest countryside on the entire trail. When he stopped at Cold Springs, he found the station burned, the attendant killed, and the horses stolen.

In a grove of trees in Old Sac, the historic section of Sacramento, a bronze rider sits astride a rearing horse. "This statue commemorates the glory of the Pony Express, which started here at 2:45 a.m. on April 14, 1860," the plaque begins. The mail had arrived late by steamship, forcing the rider to begin in the middle of the night in a downpour. All along the line, riders pushed to make up the time. With a few minutes to spare, the mail arrived in St. Joseph in exactly ten days. At almost the same time, the westbound mail arrived in Sacramento. The Pony Express worked. And it kept working, even with money hemorrhaging from every link in the system. When the overland telegraph was completed in October of 1861, the Pony's days were over.

During its 18 months of service the Pony Express delivered 35,000 pieces of mail, with the loss of only one mochila. It kept California connected with the East during the early months of the Civil War—among its deliveries was the text of Lincoln's Inaugural Address, transported in a record 7 days 17 hours.

Part of the romance of the Pony Express is that it was so short-lived—it was outmoded almost as soon as the first hoofbeats faded from the streets of St. Joe. And the other part? Bravery. Pure and simple. ◆

A restored Pony Express station in Gothenburg, Nebraska, exudes both age and beauty.

CHAPTER 10

NEZ PERCE
(NEE-ME-POO)
TRAIL

A monument commemorates the Bear Paw Battlefield where Chief Joseph and the Nez Perce made
their final stand in northern Montana in 1877. A distant rainbow brightens the somber scene.

CANADA
U.S.

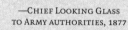

Leave us alone. We are living here peacefully and want no trouble.

—CHIEF LOOKING GLASS
TO ARMY AUTHORITIES, 1877

Twelve years after the Civil War ended, Americans were again killing each other. The United States Army, carrying out orders it did not uniformly agree with, hounded a faction of nearly 800 Nez Perce men, women, and children through 1,200 rugged miles of Idaho, Wyoming, and Montana. Four months of battles and skirmishes ended only 40 miles shy of Canada and escape. It was one of the last and most heartbreaking of the Indian wars. Several hundred people died, and the Army's victory rang drum-hollow, leaving many soldiers haunted for the rest of their lives by what they had seen and done.

Except for the Iditarod, none of the other national historic trails traverse such consistently unaltered scenery. And none but the Trail of Tears has such a sad tale to tell. Like the Mormon Trail, it honors a persecuted group. But the Mormons, who started 30 years earlier, found their self-proclaimed promised land; the Nez Perce were left with nowhere to go. Beauty amid sorrow, then, is the hallmark of the Nez Perce (Nee-Me-Poo) Trail. Its grassy valleys, sage-covered foothills, and breathtaking ranges only accentuate the poignancy of the story.

This trail can be approached as one would a medieval labyrinth, meditatively and with reverence, and not necessarily going from start to finish. In fact, Nez Perce National Historical Park is a constellation of some 38 scattered sites—more a concept than a place

Jackson Sundown, a champion rodeo rider and member of the Nez Perce tribe, proudly sits astride his steed in 1918.

with boundaries. Running through it, with the haphazard physics of war, is the trail itself. What begins to emerge as you tour these sites is a picture of a people who were not confined to one park-size area—that is, until forced by an avalanche of miners and settlers to a smaller and smaller reservation. Finally, cornered, they fought back.

Today, 62 percent of the Nez Perce Trail passes through privately owned land. About 20 percent lies in national forests, 7 percent in national parks, 6 percent within the Bureau of Land Management, and 5 percent in state lands. So sizable sections of it remain accessible, though often difficult to reach, and the precise route is largely conjecture. An autoroute approximates the whole journey, touching down at key places and offering an overall look at the region.

The Nez Perce story begins with an 1855 treaty that guaranteed them a seven-million-acre chunk of Washington, Oregon, and Idaho—most of their original homeland. But with the discovery of gold on the reservation a few years later, thousands of miners flooded in. The federal government demanded a new

Sunlight reflects off Idaho's Salmon River. While encamped in a canyon near the river, the Nez Perce were attacked by the U.S. cavalry. The Indians routed the larger force.

treaty in 1863, one that squeezed the reservation down to a tenth of its size. Five bands of Nez Perce refused to sign and continued to live where they always had. But by 1877, the Indian Bureau bowed to settlers' demands and ordered the nontreaty Nez Perce to move into the reduced reservation within 30 days. Despite the difficulty of moving all their livestock and possessions, the nontreaties began to comply.

But on June 15, three of their young warriors killed several settlers in revenge for earlier killings. Other Indians, emotions at the boiling point, joined in. Within two days, 19 settlers were dead. All this at the hands of the Nez Perce, who had aided Lewis and Clark in 1805 and had been known ever since for their friendliness toward whites. They decided to run. Giving chase, the U.S. Army was in for a deadly surprise.

The Indians fled south from a place called Camas Prairie to the canyon country of the Salmon River. On the morning of June 17, expecting an attack, some 70 warriors positioned themselves in the ravines and brushy knolls around what is now called

A lone buffalo skull on the northern Montana prairie is a haunting reminder of the days when millions of bison swarmed over the Great Plains. White hunters and pioneers decimated the once mighty herds.

White Bird Creek. Meanwhile, 106 largely inexperienced cavalrymen were riding into the death trap. Although the Indians sent out a truce flag, they were shot at. The battle had begun. Within hours, the army detachment was destroyed—34 soldiers lay dead. The Nez Perce had not lost a single warrior; furthermore, carbines, pistols, and ammunition littered the battlefield—an arsenal that would sustain the Indians for months to come.

Today horizon-to-horizon wheat fields stretch across the Camas Prairie, south of Grangeville, Idaho, where Nez Perce once dug for nutritional camas bulbs. A few miles south, US 95 summits 4,245-foot White Bird Hill. Beyond lies a convoluted land-scape of hills and rolling grasslands, a rich tapestry of velvet browns and greens. To the east, a winding country road explores White Bird Battlefield and a 1.5-mile walking trail takes you around the hillocks and steep rocky cliffs that saw military action more than a century ago. There is no visitor center and only minor tourism, with few people bothering to descend from the overlooks on the highway. Quiet breezes nudge tussocky grasses, and sharp-shinned hawks patrol the skies. Just west of the highway, the Salmon River winds around to the Snake and the popular Hells Canyon National Recreation Area, while to the east lies a vast complex of designated wilderness and

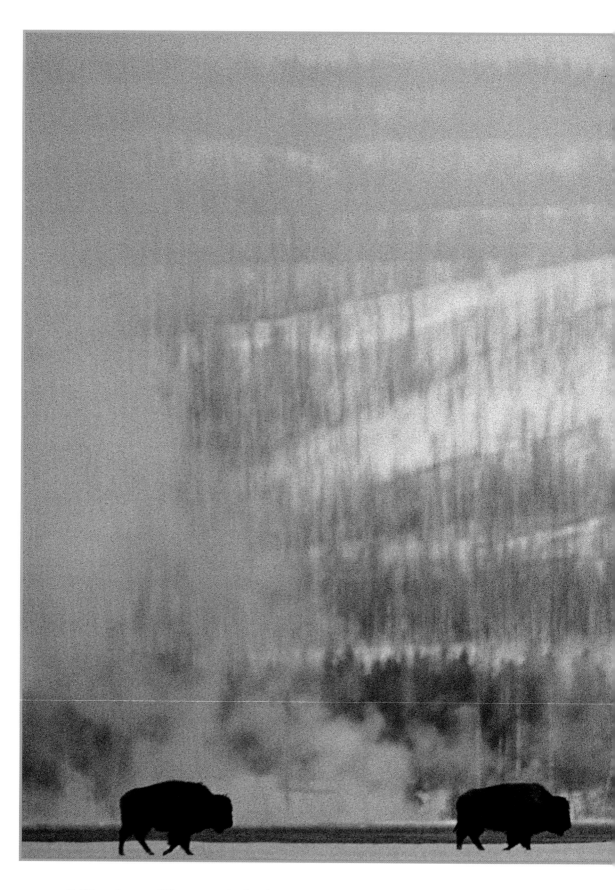

Buffalo trudge across Yellowstone National Park's Lamar Valley. The park was established in 1872; five years later,

the U.S. Army pursued the Nez Perce through the park and the beleaguered Indians seized several tourists as hostages.

Lying motionless in the Montana grassland, an elk fawn awaits the return of its mother who is off foraging. Mature elk grow to formidable size; adult males can weigh 1,100 pounds.

national forest lands. White Bird, in other words, lies within a region that has changed little in the 125 years since the battle.

For a month the Nez Perce played cat and mouse with the army. Several inconclusive skirmishes convinced the Indians they would never be left alone. The army called for reinforcements and even recruited settlers in an effort to hem in the Nez Perce. The five bands finally decided to head east over the Lolo Trail to buffalo country in Montana, where they hoped to join their Crow allies and live in peace far from white settlement. But the Crows did not welcome them, and in fact only tried to steal their horses. As for the "buffalo country," it didn't exist anymore. The Nez Perce knew that the numbers of buffalo had dwindled; nonetheless, they searched familiar hunting routes, hoping to find some place that would allow them to exist as they had for generations. In 1877, there was no such place.

Emerging into the Bitterroot Valley in present-day Montana, the Nez Perce made a crucial decision. Some leaders argued for heading north into Canada. Had they done so, they might have eluded capture. Instead, they went south, up the valley, marching toward the most deadly battle of the war. Thinking they would not be pursued this far beyond Idaho, they slackened their pace and sent no scouts rearward, believing that the presence of scouts would show a distrust of the peace they had made with local settlers.

On August 9, the Nez Perce were camped peacefully in tipis by the Big Hole River, just west of the present-day town of Wisdom. At first light, 162 soldiers under the command of Col. John Gibbon swept down upon the unsuspecting Indians. Joining the attackers were settlers who, until then, had been on friendly terms with the Nez Perce.

Groping about in the pre-dawn light, the Nez Perce chiefs managed to rally their warriors and put up a defense. But the damage had been done. Scores of women, children, and old people had been slaughtered, the scene unimaginable. Wails of grief and rage soon turned into war whoops—the brutality would be answered. Eventually the Nez Perce pushed the army back across the river, buried their dead, and tended to their wounded. Then they regrouped and broke to the south. Final toll: upwards of 90 Nez Perce dead, including 30 warriors; the Army lost 29 men, with 40 wounded.

Other than a paved road, visitor center, and a few park buildings, the battlefield today looks much as it did in 1877. The skeletal frames of tipi reconstructions along the river suggest not just the location of the camp, but the ghosts of the people who occupied them. The grassy vale and willow thickets, the slope of lodgepole and ponderosa pines, and the views of snowcapped peaks epitomize this trail's mingling of beauty and melancholy.

From here, small backroads—some paved, others gravel—trace the approximate route of the Indian retreat south and over the Continental Divide at Bannack Pass. Driving the ranch country and forested highlands through here you have to wonder how the crippled band of Nez Perce ever made it. They had to take their wounded, protect their families, move what belongings they could, and fight a war all at the same time.

Their riches consisted mostly of Appaloosa horses, which needed forage and tending. The Indians bartered for food and supplies; if refused, they took what they needed. Picture them coming into a white settlement with their huge herd, a whole village on the move, their chiefs reassuring fearful settlers that they only wanted safe passage. It's hard to avoid a mental image of the Nez Perce war as a band of simple people outfoxing a technologically superior force. Yet the reality, says Nez Perce Trail administrator Keith Thurlkill, was more complex: "The Nez Perce were a sophisticated people, many of whom spoke English and had gone to missionary schools. Some by that time owned cabins and businesses."

They headed up the Lemhi Valley, then east toward Wyoming amid lofty peaks and cool valleys that today still hold the promise of refuge—if not for people then at least for animals. Here in the wild-to-the-core heart of the Rockies lives a rich diversity of wildlife—grizzly bears, bighorn sheep, mountain goats, cougars, moose, and elk. A haven, even then, for many such species, Yellowstone National Park was five years old when the Nez Perce came through. A few visitors were in for more than they had planned on. Spotted by a party of nine tourists, the

Respected tribal elder, Molly Minthorn, rides in the parade at the Pendleton Round-Up in Oregon in 1921. For the annual

event, Minthorn uses an adorned woman's saddle that features a high pommel—and enough room in the back for a child.

Nez Perce felt they had to capture them. Some escaped; the rest were freed farther east in the park. Rearguard warriors later killed and wounded several other tourists and burned a ranch.

By September they were traveling north, now making a dash for Canada. In one heroic 36-hour period, the bone-weary, battle-weakened Indians pushed themselves 70 miles through the rough-and-tumble country south of the Missouri River. Why didn't their pursuers just wish them good riddance? "The Army had been chasing them for four months," explains Dan Gard, project manager for the Nez Perce Trail. "They'd suffered heavy casualties. There was no way they were going to let the Nez Perce go."

Bear Paw Battlefield lies on a pristine piece of wind-whipped Montana prairie two days' march south of Saskatchewan. A primitive walking trail investigates the key sites, including a cave where women and children took shelter. But interpretation remains minimal and visitation scarce at this remote, lonely memento mori. It was here that the Nez Perce made their final stand, enduring a six-day siege and dozens of casualties. When it was over, four of the original chiefs were dead; the fifth, White Bird, had made an escape to Canada with 200 people. It was left to Chief Joseph, who had never been a war leader, to surrender the tattered remnant—about 400 Indians. The children were freezing; other people had simply disappeared.

"I am tired," Chief Joseph said. "My heart is sick and sad. From where the sun now stands, I will fight no more forever."

But Joseph did fight, with stirring words that made him the spokesman for his people. His tireless lobbying paid off after eight years, when the Nez Perce were allowed to leave their captivity and return to the Northwest. Joseph and some others, however, were sent to a reservation in eastern Washington. Never allowed back to his homeland, Joseph died in 1904, in his early 60s. "We didn't lose," says a descendant of Joseph, Charlie Moses, Jr. "We didn't surrender. We simply quit fighting, with the promise that we'd be able to return to Idaho. I suspect that in 1877 our people didn't know what the word surrender meant. Our journey just begins at Bear Paw."

Designated in 1986, the Nez Perce Trail pays tribute to the efforts of a people to find asylum. At a time when the country was heading west, they fled eastward, looking for something that was already gone. Military experts have often praised the brilliance of the Nez Perce strategy, as though a posthumous medal of honor could soften the defeat. But for the Nez Perce, it was less a war than a desperate flight—their goal not to win, only to avoid losing. Chief Joseph said, "We were contented to let things remain as the Great Spirit made them." ◆

A Montana hillside features colorful lupines and sunflower-like balsamroot. Indians used balsamroot sap as an antiseptic.

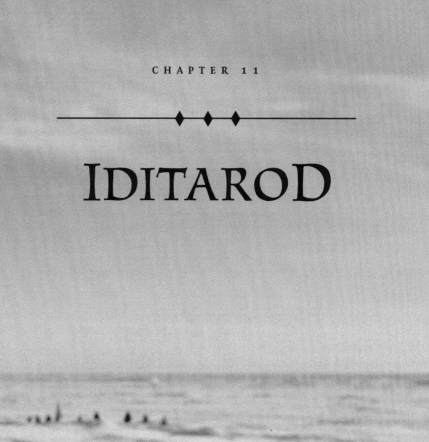

CHAPTER 11

IDITAROD

An elderly Eskimo woman gazes at the frozen landscape in Nome, Alaska. The grueling Iditarod Trail ends at Nome, the remote coastal town that was once overrun with gold-hungry prospectors.

No one who has ever run the Iditarod—or even part of it—would ever trade the experience for anything else.

—DON BOWERS, VOLUNTEER PILOT
IDITAROD AIR FORCE

Before it came to be known as a great sled race from Anchorage to Nome, it was an Alaskan town, named after a river called Iditarod, or distant place. The river still runs, but now the town is a deserted ghost so distant from civilization that the only regular way in is by floatplane. If you tried to get there in summer from the nearest highway, you would have to walk more than 300 miles of boot-sucking muskeg, forested mountains, and shrub-choked tundra. If the walk didn't kill you, swimming the cold, swift rivers might. You could wait until the Bering Sea thawed enough to get a boat up the Yukon, like some of the early miners, then travel about 500 miles upstream.

There is one other way.

When the tundra and rivers are frozen and covered with snow—in late October to early April—you hitch up a team of sled dogs in Anchorage, and in about five days of continuous travel you're there. Of course, it helps if you know the dogs and the trail as well you know your own face. But since there are no roadhouses along the way anymore, you'd be in for a survival expedition. In fact, unless you're one of the top sled-dog racers in the world, just forget about doing the 1,000-plus-mile Iditarod Trail—the wildest of the national historic trails—in anything other than an airplane.

It used to be a little easier to get to the town of Iditarod, the mid-point of the Iditarod Trail. That was when there was a reason for coming here. In its heyday as Alaska's last major gold-rush town, 2,000 people lived here; from nearby creeks,

A team of powerful sled dogs—including a startlingly blue-eyed dog—races briskly along the Iditarod Trail.

30 million dollars in gold was removed in the 1910s and 1920s. It's now a dot on the map, a scattering of tumbledown cabins and mining buildings set amid a mosaic of spruce, poplar, and tundra. Flat and monochromatic, the town is hardly scenic. What has endured is a name that is synonymous with strength and endurance—two qualities that are highly valued in this part of the country.

A network of Native American trails had been in place for hundreds of years across the interior of Alaska. They were originally used to track game, and then later used by the Ingalik and Tanaina Indians as a trade and commerce route. When the first gold stampedes hit in the 1880s, prospectors used, and sometimes even improved, many of the native trails as they headed to the goldfields. Then, in 1910, the U.S. Army's Alaska Road Commission surveyed a standard route for individuals carrying in mail, food, and supplies, and hauling out gold; it was called the Seward to Nome Mail Trail.

Although a few people did the trail by snowshoe or even bicycle or horse-drawn sled, the dogsled was the favored transportation. Following the Russian pattern, teams of 6 to 20 dogs—usually malamutes, Siberian huskies, or wolves—were harnessed in pairs, with a lead dog in front. Voice commands from French-Canadian trappers were adapted: for instance, *marche* (go ahead) became "mush." Roadhouses sprang up along the trail about 20 miles apart. Most offered basic room and board, though some provided such luxuries as a pool table and phonograph.

In the early 1920s, airplanes began taking over the mail and freight runs; at the same time, the gold mines were giving out. The Seward to Nome Mail Trail, as well as the network of paths, was becoming a snow-swirled scratch on a vast wilderness, marked by empty roadhouses and defunct mining towns. Within three decades, dogsledding was becoming a rare event—and snowmobiles were now taking people where they needed to go, relatively hassle free.

Then an event occurred that embedded itself in the national consciousness. It was the winter of 1925, and many children in Nome had been hit with diptheria. Frantic telegraph messages tracked down the only antitoxin serum in Alaska. It was in Anchorage, and the only available planes had been dismantled for the winter. So the serum was put in a cylinder, which was wrapped in a quilt and sent by rail to Nenana. It was then tied onto a dogsled for the first leg of an 18-team effort that used parts of what would later became the Iditarod Trail. In the teeth of biting gale-force winds, a blizzard, and temperatures down to 60° below 0°F, the dogs and men traveled around the clock, covering in five and a half days what would normally have taken four times as long. The children were saved, and the effort came to symbolize the tough, can-do spirit of Alaska.

Perhaps it was no surprise, then, that in 1967 historian Dorothy Page and musher Joe Redington, Sr., chose a 60-mile dog race over part of the old Seward to Nome Mail Trail as a way to celebrate the Alaska Purchase

A hiker views the snow bound Crow Pass southeast of Anchorage. Part of the original Iditarod Trail that led to Alaskan goldfields, this mountain pass is now traversed by outdoor enthusiasts.

centennial. Six years later, the race was extended more than 1,000 miles between two of Alaska's most economically important cities, Anchorage and Nome. Twenty-two mushers finished that year. Since then, more than 1,300 have completed the Iditarod Sled Dog Race, the "last great race on Earth."

In 1978, old mail and gold-rush paths, linked to the Seward to Nome Mail Trail by the sled dog race, became one of the first four designated national historic trails. Including all its shortcuts and alternate race routes, the Iditarod National Historic Trail today comprises more than 2,450 miles. Though most of the trail crosses public land, the Iditarod has one of the most

complex patterns of ownership of any national trail. The only one administered by the Bureau of Land Management, the Iditarod passes through lands owned by municipal governments, native corporations, the state of Alaska, the U.S. government, and private citizens. No less than ten institutional land managers include the U.S. Fish and Wildlife Service, the U.S. Forest Service, and the Department of Defense.

What does all that mean for recreational users? The issue of the trail's ownership pales in comparison with its physical difficulty. We're not talking about a blazed walking path with signposts and shelters. The Iditarod is a howling ocean of frozen tundra

Sled dogs easily outnumber people in this early view of downtown Seward, Alaska. Dogsleds were the primary mode of

transportation into the Alaskan interior from this port town on Resurrection Bay until a railroad was built in the early 1900s.

Following the historic route of the Iditarod, the Alaska Railroad Corporation travels through scenic wilderness areas inaccessible by car.

and iced mountains that happens to have once been a link to civilization. Since it's not a "trail" in the usual sense, most people are content to hike, ski, snowmobile, and mountain bike the miles and miles of wilderness accessible from the small communities. The lack of fuel, shelter, and supplies makes an end-to-end journey for the casual tourist is all but impossible—that is why most know the trail in terms of the Iditarod race. "There are people who do offer tours," says trail administrator Mike Zaidlicz, "but generally going from beginning to end is just too daunting a prospect. Most people will go about a hundred yards before they turn around and decide there's something better they can do."

For training, British and U.S. Special Forces have attempted the trail under some of the worst conditions without uniform success. On the other hand, a group of Boy Scouts with help from scattered villages and under good conditions had no problem. Every year some 10 to 20 recreationists try the entire trail; many end up being rescued.

The first section of the Iditarod Trail, which is not part of the race, is the only part you can tour by paved road. This 200 or so miles from Seward to Knik also happen to hold some of the most splendid scenery on the entire trail. Up the Kenai Peninsula and around Turnagain Arm, the highway unfolds a constantly changing panorama of snow-crested mountains and sparkling bodies of water. Since you're on a highway, it's not exactly wild, but there are long stretches between towns and plenty of places to get out for short walks.

Milepost zero on the trail stands in the ice-free port town of Seward. A railroad into the interior was begun here in 1903, but while that was ongoing, dogs were still the main link to points north. With its spectacular setting on mountain-rimmed Resurrection Bay, Seward would seem a likely candidate for a resort town. A 130-mile scenic highway connects it with Anchorage, making it an easy weekend getaway. But, though many people come to fish and

A conductor for the Alaska Railroad Corporation summons travelers to board the train that is about to leave the station at Seward, Alaska.

take a peek at the nearby glaciers, Seward maintains a small-town look and feel. Other than cruises, commercialism is low here. Perhaps it has to do with the weather—the standard Alaskan recipe of five parts cloudy to one part sunny, with maybe three days a year when shorts come in handy.

The best place to get a sense of the Iditarod near Seward is the 14-mile trail just north of town. Cleared by the Forest Service and the Iditarod Trail Blazers, the trail passes through a forest of hemlock and sitka spruce around Bear Lake. Moose browse the underbrush, while waterfowl set their wings over the area's many lakes. Sightings of black bears and grizzlies are not uncommon. Up near Girdwood, several miles of the old trail were recently discovered and cleared. A corridor of alder—an early succession tree—shooting through an old-growth forest was the clue; trail workers then began noticing logs from the old corduroy road hidden under mats of moss. Just north, a 27-mile trail cuts through the half-million-acre expanse of Chugach State Park. Dall's sheep, mountain goats, and lynx are a few inhabitants of this wilderness of alpine meadows and jagged, snowy peaks.

Though Anchorage, established in 1915, was not around in the early years of the trail, it has become the starting point for the annual race. Thousands of spectators line the streets on the first Saturday in March for the festivities. Yet the race does not officially begin here. The dogsled teams, usually about 60, make a ceremonial start downtown, then mush some 15 miles to the town of Eagle River, where the dogs are loaded into trucks. The following day, the timed race begins in Wasilla, 40 miles north of Anchorage, and far enough from the busy highway system that from here

A musher urges on his team as they traverse Rainy Pass that crosses the Alaska Range. The highest point on the trail at

3,000 plus feet, the route then drops steeply 1,000 feet in 5 miles to become a treacherous stretch where many sleds overturn.

on they have an unimpeded run to Nome. Mushers can start with as many as 16 dogs and end with as few as 5, but substitutions are not allowed. To insure a fair race, veterinarians at some 20 checkpoints use hand-held scanners to check the ID microchips implanted in the dogs' ears. Also, sick or worn-out dogs are pulled and sent home.

After Knik, the trail enters a roadless wilderness and stays there until just outside Nome. At 3,350 feet, Rainy Pass marks the high point of the Iditarod, where it sneaks through the mighty Alaska Range. The highest mountain on the continent, Mount McKinley lies only 75 air miles north. Many spectators fly to Finger Lake near the pass to take in the excitement of the race at one of its most visually stunning places.

West of the Alaska Range the trail begins descending to the river-incised flats that tilt toward the Bering Sea. To give a brief economic burst to isolated villages, the race alternates each year between a southern and northern route from Takotna to Kaltag. With the infusion of support personnel, media, and tourists, communities of a few hundred people or less can suddenly double in size.

From Kaltag on the Yukon River, the trail heads to the 2,000-year-old Yupik Eskimo village of Unalakleet. At this point, the Iditarod shoots north, wrapping around the edge of Norton Sound, which in winter is frozen solid. The Bering Sea, in fact, can be frozen for more than 300 miles out from shore, blocking water access for eight months. The winter sun spills its faint light from the horizon for a few hours

and then disappears. Some of the country's unique wildlife call this area home—arctic hares, musk oxen, reindeer, caribou, walrus, and the occasional polar bear.

The rocky bluffs of Nome signal trail's end and provide visual relief from the unrelenting flatness of the landscape all around. It was on these remote beaches that gold was discovered in 1898. From a peak population of 20,000—at one time the highest in the state—the size of Nome has dwindled to around 3,500. Mining and tourism are the town's chief enterprises. A gravel road heading east parallels the trail along the coast for about 30 miles, though its main purpose is to connect Nome with a couple of smaller communities.

When the dog teams reach Nome, a fragile connection has been reforged. "There's a certain beauty to living 500 miles from any interconnecting highway system in the world," says Nome resident Leo Rasmussen, "and that's what the Iditarod National Historic Trail does for us—it amplifies that beauty. It's the only real land-based transportation that takes place to Nome anymore."

Linking Alaska's east with its west, its past with its present—the Iditarod Trail is valued today not for how many people it brings across America's last great wild place, but for how few. ◆

Swathed in low-lying fog, the Chugach
Mountains rise in a wilderness area next to
Anchorage, Alaska's largest city.

CHAPTER 12

SELMA TO MONTGOMERY

Hoisting American flags, civil rights activists march between Selma and Montgomery, Alabama. Beaten during their first attempt, the marchers succeeded in reaching the state capitol on March 25, 1965. Congress passed the Voting Rights Act five months later.

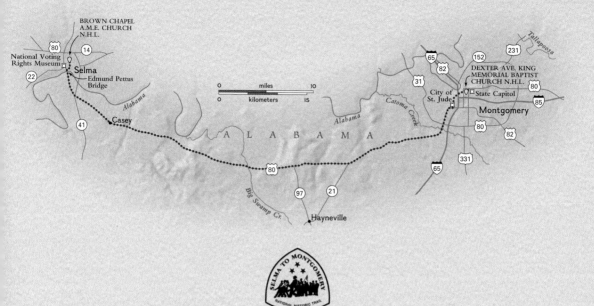

How long? Not long, because no lie can live forever.... How long? Not long. Because the arm of the moral universe is long but it bends toward justice.

—MARTIN LUTHER KING, JR., 1965

Thus spoke Martin Luther King, Jr., in front of the Alabama State Capitol after leading the 54-mile, voting-rights march from Selma. The shortest and most recent of the national historic trails was a long time coming. A full century went by from the time the Civil War ended until the Selma to Montgomery march occurred. As a direct result of that march, Congress passed the Voting Rights Act that protected the right of black people to vote in federal, state, and local elections. A shining example of King's doctrine of social change through nonviolent protest, the march was considered the high-water mark of the civil rights movement of the 1950s and '60s. In 1996, the Selma to Montgomery route was designated a national historic trail.

The march took place from March 21-25, 1965, but to set the scene we need to wind back a couple of months:

January 2, 1965. Dr. King and members of the Southern Christian Leadership Conference arrive in Selma and hold a rally at Brown Chapel African Methodist Episcopal Church. The rally itself violates a county ordinance passed the previous summer, banning meetings of more than three people. The law's intention is to prevent "outside agitators" from stirring up trouble in Selma. But locals themselves requested help, because despite new civil rights laws they are still kept off the voting registers— poll taxes, arcane tests, and outright intimidation cut the black voting population down to 2 percent of its potential. Nearby counties have even fewer blacks registered.

Policemen in helmets line the steps of the state capitol in Montgomery, Alabama, in March 1965.

Selma's National Voting Rights Museum looks out upon the Edmund Pettus Bridge, the site where state troopers and the local sheriff's posse set upon peaceful marchers. The names of civil rights activists emblazon the windows.

February 18, 1965. Tensions are high in Selma, Montgomery, and nearby towns. Mass meetings and marches have led to violence and multiple arrests. After a night march in the town of Marion, protesters leave Zion Methodist Church; state troopers move in and attack. One witness recalls troopers shooting out streetlights and destroying a television camera. In the pandemonium, people run to a café for protection. There, 26-year-old Jimmie Lee Jackson is shot while trying to protect his mother and grandfather. In the hospital a week later, he dies.

March 7, 1965. More than 500 people march across the Edmund Pettus Bridge in Selma. Awaiting them just beyond the town limits are state troopers and a mounted posse of deputized local citizens. The marchers are told to disperse. When they refuse, the troopers charge, using tear gas and billy clubs to chase the marchers all the way back across the bridge to Brown Chapel. This time the event is captured on camera. Broadcast all over the nation, "Bloody Sunday" generates tremendous sympathy for the movement.

March 9, 1965. Four white men attack James Reeb, a white Unitarian minister from Boston who supported civil rights. After he leaves a Selma restaurant, they beat him in the head. He dies two days later.

March 15, 1965. President Johnson comes out in favor of voting rights legislation. "At times," he says, "history and fate meet at a single time, in a single place to shape a turning point in man's unending search for freedom. So it was at Lexington and Concord. So it was a century ago at Appomattox. So it was last week in Selma, Alabama."

March 21, 1965. Under protection of the National Guard, some 3,000 marchers set out from Brown Chapel and head east. A federal court order limits the marchers to 300 along the two-lane section of US 80. Four days later the procession reaches the capitol in Montgomery and the crowd swells to 25,000. Dr. King and others give speeches, while Governor George Wallace watches from an office window. That night, Viola Liuzzo, a white housewife from Detroit, is shot to death by Klansmen as she shuttles marchers back to Selma.

August 6, 1965. President Johnson signs the Voting Rights Act into law.

If you walk the streets of Selma today, you find it hard to believe that the eyes of the world were focused here 36 years ago. Situated on a bluff above the Alabama River, Selma is anybody's vision of a quiet Southern town. Along Water Street, painted brick warehouses have been converted to

Mrs. Robert Gardner holds a civil-rights-era photo of her husband with a church group. The Gardners bravely allowed activists to camp on their property during the 1965 march.

unpretentious restaurants and antique shops, antebellum manses preserve generations of family lore on leafy side streets, and people still say hello to strangers. Yet a sense of unfinished business lingers here. For every spruced-up building with ornamental ironwork downtown, there's another that's boarded up or in need of repair. A few years ago, the scene was nearly the same. You almost have the impression that construction work takes place maybe once a week, and then everybody takes off to go fishing or find better employment elsewhere. Progress occurs, but slowly.

Turn the corner at Water and walk down Martin Luther King Jr. Street, where the city has devised a "historic walking tour," complete with brochure and sidewalk markers. With its disorienting juxtaposition of recent history and stark reality, this has to be one of the most fascinating walking tours in the country. Along these three blocks stand the Brown Chapel African Methodist Episcopal Church, a 1906 Byzantine-style beauty, and the 1896 First Baptist Church—both of them the scene of major rallies in the 1960s. Along here, as well, are the squat brick buildings of a 1950s housing complex, where part of Selma's

Martin Luther King, Jr., and his wife, Coretta, lead protesters in Selma, Alabama, in March 1965. Some 25,000 people

demanding voting rights for blacks converged on the state capitol in Montgomery, many walking 54 miles from Selma.

58 percent black population lives. Laundry hangs in public yards, and piles of trash fester in abandoned lots. Yet tidy flower gardens also flourish here, where, as one information panel points out, marchers in the '60s were drilled in tactics of nonviolent confrontation.

Though slick tourism may never gloss Selma, the town could ironically find itself pulled from an economic slump by the very people it once subjugated. On the wrong side of history when it functioned as a major arsenal of the Confederacy, Selma was dragged kicking and screaming to the other side a century later. By 1972, five blacks had been elected to the Selma City Council. And in 2000, James Perkins, Jr., became the city's first black mayor by unseating nine-term Mayor Joe Smitherman, who began his first term in 1964. In a sense, Selma is still making history today.

Opened in 1993, the National Voting Rights Museum is by far Selma's top tourist attraction. It commemorates the movement with photographs, films, and memorabilia. Glass cases containing chains and clubs serve as reminders of the brutality meted out by local officialdom. But the most powerful exhibit is a wall-length mirror covered with Post-it notes that contain handwritten testimonials. Most writers pen only a few lines: "I got stomped by the state troopers' horses in the back of Edmund Pettus Bridge...." "I was jailed in Marion for demonstrating...." Others recall being tear-gassed, cattle-prodded, billy-clubbed.

Some mention the good food and entertainment at the overnight camps. People drop in almost daily to add their stories.

Museum tour director Joanne Bland was 11 years old at the time of the march, and she participated in the first and last legs, as well as the Bloody Sunday event. "I had never experienced violence," she says. "Violence was remote—it was in Mississippi, it was in Arkansas, it was in Birmingham. Never here in Selma. . . . The last I remembered was seeing a policeman on horseback running full speed at this lady. And it was just too much for me. I fainted, and I woke up on the other side of the bridge. My sister who was 14 years old was leaning over me in the back of a car and she was crying and stuff was dropping on my face. And when I came fully awake I realized it wasn't tears—it was her blood. She had been beaten on the bridge."

After the civil rights movement, Bland spent 20 years away from Selma, then returned here to live. "One of the things that I like so much about Selma," she says, "is that it looks virtually the same as it did in the '60s. The difference is inside the buildings. Before, 99 percent of the businesses were owned by whites, and blacks worked for them. Now you see a happy mixture of black and white businesses alongside each other. But I don't want anyone to think that I think we've arrived, because we have not here in Selma. We still struggle. It's very hard to interject change in a place that was so adamant about not changing."

Cheerleaders cross the Edmund Pettus Bridge on a peaceful day in Selma. On Sunday March 7, 1965, state troopers and a local posse violently attacked voting rights activists trying to march across the bridge. The courage of the protesters has not been forgotten by a new generation. "We can vote. We can go where we want to go," says Shameecka Perkins at far right. "The people that made that possible are my heroes."

On the south side of Selma, the Edmund Pettus Bridge still crosses the broad, kudzu-lined Alabama River. You can walk across it if you like, though traffic presses close to the sidewalk. But from here to Montgomery, the historic trail is manageable only by car. It's a lovely drive on US 80 through the gently rolling topography of the Black Belt, a swath of middle Alabama floored with rich, dark soil that has yielded countless tons of cotton. Trees draped in gauzy Spanish moss line the road, while wide green pastures stretch into the distance. The marchers' ancestors worked some of these same fields as slaves. Brown

signs along the highway indicate the campsites at various farms.

The final campsite was at the City of St. Jude, a social welfare complex on the outskirts of Montgomery. Set up by the Roman Catholic Church, St. Jude includes schools, a church, a convent, and a hospital that has been renovated into an apartment building for the elderly. The highway at this point becomes a busy thoroughfare of traffic lights and shopping centers before entering a low-income residential section of the city.

Though recent years have improved its appearance, downtown Montgomery, like Selma, still exists in something of a time

A windshield reflects Brown Chapel African Methodist Episcopal Church. From the church's pulpit, Martin

Luther King, Jr., thundered, "We are not on our knees begging for the ballot, we are demanding the ballot."

warp. Parking meters are still a nickel an hour, and cappuccino has yet to find its way into the local vernacular. But one noticeable difference is that, thanks to Rosa Parks and others who risked their jobs to participate in the 1955-1956 bus boycott, anybody can sit anywhere on the public buses. With its high-tech multimedia exhibits, the new Rosa Parks Library and Museum vividly re-creates the boycott story, though a virtual-ride polish creates a distancing from events that happened only 45 years ago.

More telling is to walk up to Dexter Avenue King Memorial Baptist Church, where Martin Luther King, Jr., served as pastor from 1954 to 1960. From here you have a straight-on view of the dazzling, white state capitol two blocks away, dominating the city like a Greek Revival plantation house. A bronze star on its marble steps marks where Jefferson Davis took the oath of office as President of the Confederacy, and where governors are still sworn in—holding Davis's Bible. It was also on these steps that the 1965 Selma to Montgomery march ended. Standing here, you feel a profound sense of the ironies of American history. The Confederate flag was removed from the capitol dome in 1992, but another still waves prominently atop a Confederate monument at the north entrance. Inscriptions honor the old South. To wit: "The knightliest of the knightly race who singe the days of old, have kept the lamp of chivalry alight in hearts of gold."

A block away, the First White House of the Confederacy is where Jefferson Davis lived for the first three months of his tenure. Cameron Napier, regent of the White House Association and sixth generation Montgomerian, weaves a balance between extreme views found in the city: "Anybody who speaks up for Confederacy, immediately people are going to think, 'Oh, they're racist.' And that's not so. It's point counterpoint; you can't have one without the other."

Two blocks east, an armed guard patrols the Civil Rights Memorial around the clock. Vandals once spilled paint on the memorial; more importantly, the memorial's founder, who started the adjacent Southern Poverty Law Center, has received death threats for prosecuting members of the Ku Klux Klan. But, in fact, the guard sees very little action. Designed by Maya Lin of Vietnam Veterans Memorial fame, the memorial features a black granite table from which water bubbles out, flowing over the names of 40 people murdered during the civil rights movement. Groups of schoolchildren, black and white, often visit this serene plaza. They put their hands in the water and touch the engraved names.

Montgomery represents a confluence in the stream of American history, a flowing together of black and white, Civil War and civil rights. To travel the short distance from Selma is to see clearly that ours is a shared history, irrevocably entwined. ◆

Proud veteran of the five-day march from Selma to Montgomery, Marie Foster wears the safety vest, signed by fellow marchers, that she used on the trek.

ADDITIONAL TRAIL INFORMATION

◆ ◆ ◆

Below are addresses, agency names, phone numbers,
and Web locations for the historic trails included in this book.

JUAN BAUTISTA DE ANZA

Amigos de Anza
1350 Castle Rock Rd., Walnut Canyon, CA 94598 (510) 926-1081
Anza Trail Coalition of Arizona
PO Box 42612, Tucson, AZ 85733-2612
Juan Bautista de Anza National Historic Trails
1111 Jackson St., #700, Oakland, CA 94607
(510) 817-1438; *www.nps.gov/juba/*

OVERMOUNTAIN VICTORY

Overmountain Victory Trail Association
1651 West Elk Ave., Elizabethton, TN 37643
(423) 543-5808; *www.ovta.org*
National Park Service Southeast Regional Office
Atlanta Federal Center, 1924 Building 100 Alabama St.,
SW, Atlanta, GA 30303
(404) 562-3124; *www.nps.gov/ovvi*

LEWIS & CLARK

National Park Service Lewis and Clark National Historic Trail
1709 Jackson St., Omaha, NE 68102
(402) 514-9311; *www.nps.gov/lecl/*
Lewis and Clark Trail Heritage Foundation, Inc.
PO Box 3434, Great Falls, MT 59403
(406) 454-1234; *www.lewisandclark.org*

SANTA FE

Santa Fe Trail Association
Santa Fe Trail Center, Rte. 3, Larned, KS 67550
(316) 285-2054; *www.nmhu.edu/research/sftrail/sfta.html*
National Park Service Long Distance Trails—Santa Fe
PO Box 728, Santa Fe, NM 87504
(505) 988-6888; *www.nps.gov/safe*

TRAIL OF TEARS

National Park Service Long Distance Trails—Santa Fe
PO Box 728, Santa Fe, NM 87504
(505) 988-6888; *www.nps.gov/safe*
American Indian Center of Arkansas
1100 N. University, #133, Little Rock, AR 72207
Trail of Tears Association Membership
PO Box 2069, Cherokee, NC 28719

OREGON

Oregon-California Trails Association
PO Box 1019, Independence, MO 64051-0519
(816) 252-2276; *www.OCTA-trails.org*
National Park Service Long-Distance Trails—Salt Lake City
324 S. State St., PO Box 45155, Salt Lake City, UT 84145-0155
(801) 539-4095;. *www.nps.gov/oreg*

CALIFORNIA

Oregon-California Trails Association
PO Box 1019, Independence, MO 64051-0519
(816) 252-2276; *www.OCTA-trails.org*
National Park Service Long-Distance Trails—Salt Lake City
324 S. State St., PO Box 45155, Salt Lake City, UT 84145
(801) 539-4095 or -4094; *www.nps.gov/cal*

MORMON PIONEER

Mormon Trails Association
300 S. Rio Grande, Salt Lake City, UT 84101
(801) 538-6983; *www.history.utah.org/partners/mta*
National Park Service Long-Distance Trails—Salt Lake City
324 S. State St., PO Box 45155, Salt Lake City, UT 84145-0155
(801) 539-4095; *www.nps.gov/mopi*

PONY EXPRESS

National Park Service Long-Distance Trails—Salt Lake City
324 S. State St., PO Box 45155, Salt Lake City, UT 84145
(801) 539-4095; *www.nps.gov/poex/*
National Pony Express Trails Association
PO Box 236 Pollock Pines, CA 95726
www.gorp.com/gorp/publishers/fulcrum/pony_exg.htm

NEZ PERCE (NEE-ME-POO)

Nez Perce National Historic Trail Foundation
PO Box 1939, Lewiston, ID 83501
(435) 655-3210; *www.public.iastate.edu/ffisfr/npnhtf/npnhtf.html*
Nez Perce National Historical Park
Rte. 1, Box 100, Highway 95, Spalding, ID 83540
(208) 843-2261; *www.halcyon.com/rdpayne/npmo.html*

IDITAROD

Anchorage District, Bureau of Land Management
6681 Abbott Loop Rd., Anchorage, AK 99507
(907) 267-1246
Iditarod Trail Committee
PO Box 870800, Wasilla, AK 99687
(907) 376-5155

SELMA TO MONTGOMERY

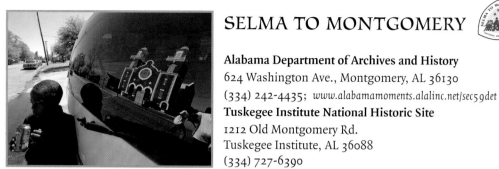

Alabama Department of Archives and History
624 Washington Ave., Montgomery, AL 36130
(334) 242-4435; *www.alabamamoments.alalinc.net/sec59det*
Tuskegee Institute National Historic Site
1212 Old Montgomery Rd.
Tuskegee Institute, AL 36088
(334) 727-6390

RECENTLY DESIGNATED NATIONAL HISTORIC TRAILS

ALA KAHAKAI

E Mau Na Ala Hele
PO Box 6110, Kamuela, HI
National Park Service Pacific-Great Basin—California
1111 Jackson St., #700, Oakland, CA 94607
(510) 817-1446

EL CAMINO REAL
DE TIERRA ADENTRO

El Camino Real Project
439 Camino Monte Vista, Santa Fe, NM 87505
(505) 982-2175
Bureau of Land Management
226 Cruz Alta Rd., Taos, NM 87571
(505) 438-7542

GENERAL INFORMATION

America's National Trails System *www.fs.fed.us/recreation/trails/natl_trails.shtml*
National Trails System Map and Guide *www.nps.gov/htdocs1/pub_aff/naltrail.htm*
National Scenic Trails *www.gorp.com/gorp/resource/us_trail/nattrail.htm*
National Historic Trails *www.gorp.com/gorp/resource/us_trail/historic.htm*
American Hiking Society 1422 Fenwick Lane, Silver Spring, MD 20910 (301) 565-6704 *www.americanhiking.org*
American Trails PO Box 11046, Prescott, AZ 86304-1046 (520) 632-5235 *www.americantrails.org*

Illustration Credits

COVER, Rich Reid/Colors of Nature; 1, Tom Bean; 2-3, Courtesy of the Anschutz Collection; 4-5, Jeff Schultz/AlaskaStock.com; 6-7, Joel Sartore/www.joelsartore.com; 8-9, Rich Reid/Colors of Nature; 10-11, John Lambing; 15, Rich Reid/Colors of Nature; 16-17, Rich Reid/Colors of Nature; 19, Rich Reid/Colors of Nature; 20, The British Library Picture Library; 21, Rich Reid/Colors of Nature; 22-23, Rich Reid/Colors of Nature; 24, Rich Reid/Colors of Nature; 25, William Ahrendt; 26-27, Rich Reid/Colors of Nature; 29, Rich Reid/Colors of Nature; 30-31, Randy Wells/stone; 33, Jim Hargan; 34, Courtesy National Park Service; 35, David Muench/ Corbis; 36-37, Andy Thomas/Maze Creek Studio/ www.andythomas.com/ 1-800-432-1581; 38, Jim Hargan; 39, Jim Hargan; 40-41, Jim Hargan; 43, Charles Gurche; 44-45, Raymond Gehman; 47, Tom Bean; 48, Amon Carter Museum of Western Art, Artwork by Lee Angle; 49, Joel Sartore/www.joelsartore.com; 50-51, John Lambing; 52, Tom Bean; 55, John Lambing; 56-57, Jeff Gnass; 59, Jeff Gnass; 60-61, Tom Bean; 63, H.F. Schmidt; 64, Bruce Hucko; 66-67, Bruce Dale; 68, Bruce Dale; 69, David Muench; 70-71, George H. H. Huey; 73, George H. H. Huey; 74-75, Linda Guerrant; 77, Phil Schermeister; 78, Linda Guerrant; 79, Phil Schermeister; 80-81, Phil Schermeister; 82, Painting by Robert Lindneux, Woolaroc Museum, Bartlesville, OK; 83, Phil Schermeister; 84-85, Linda Guerrant; 87, Charles Gurche; 88-89, Phil Schermeister; 91, Phil Schermeister; 92, Charles Gurche; 93, Phil Schermeister; 94-95, J. Maxwell Moran Collection; 97, Phil Schermeister; 98-99, Phil Schermeister; 100, Phil Schermeister; 101, Phil Schermeister; 103, Phil Schermeister; 104-105, Jim Richardson; 107, Jeff Gnass; 108, Phil Schermeister; 110-111, Courtesy The Abimlich Champion Family; 112, Phil Schermeister; 113, Phil Schermeister; 114-115, Jim Richardson; 116, Knoedler Art Galleries; 117, Jeff Gnass; 119, Phil Schermeister; 120-121, Phil Schermeister; 123, Phil Schermeister; 124, Phil Schermeister; 125, LDS Church Archives; 126-127, Museum of Church History and Art; 128, Phil Schermeister; 130-131, Phil Schermeister; 132, Phil Schermeister; 133, Museum of Church History and Art; 135, Phil Schermeister; 136-137, Phil Schermeister; 139, Marilyn Mofford Gibbons; 140, Phil Schermeister; 141, St. Joseph Museum; 142-143, Fort Laramie Archives; 145, Phil Schermeister; 146-147, Phil Schermeister; 149, Phil Schermeister; 150-151, Tom Bean; 153, Courtesy National Park Service, Nez Perce National Historic Park; 154, Charles Gurche; 155, John Lambing; 156-157, Joel Sartore/www.joelsartore.com; 158, Joel Sartore/www.joelsartore.com; 160-161, Courtesy National Park Service, Nez Perce National Historic Park; 163, John Lambing; 164-165, Jeff Schultz/AlaskaStock.com; 167, Jeff Schultz/AlaskaStock.com; 169, Richard Moran/AlaskaStock.com; 170-171, Anchorage Museum Archives; 172, Rich Reid/Colors of Nature; 173, Rich Reid/Colors of Nature; 174-175, Jeff Schultz/AlaskaStock.com; 177, Vance Gese/AlaskaStock.com; 178-179, Matt Heron/Black Star; 181, Hulton/Archive/Getty Images; 182, Meria Joel Carstarphen; 183, Meria Joel Carstarphen; 184-185, Hulton/Archive/Getty Images; 187, Meria Joel Carstarphen; 188-189, Meria Joel Carstarphen; 191, Meria Joel Carstarphen; 192, (top-bottom) Rich Reid/Colors of Nature; Steven Weinberg/stone; John Lambing; 193, (top-bottom) George H.H. Huey; Phil Schermeister; Phil Schermeister; Phil Schermeister; 194, (top-bottom) Phil Schermeister; Phil Schermeister; Joel Sartore/www.joelsartore.com; Jeff Schultz/AlaskaStock.com; 195, (top-bottom) Meria Joel Carstarphen; Helen Scully, NPS; Zandria Muench Beraldo; BACKCOVER, (top left) Phil Schermeister; (top right) Rich Reid/Colors of Nature; (bottom left) Linda Guerrant; (bottom right) John Lambing

JOHN THOMPSON is the author of five National Geographic books, including two volumes of the "America's Outdoors" series. He has written numerous articles on travel and natural history, and is a featured expert for National Geographic Expeditions. His travels for this book took him across the breadth of the entire continent. He lives with his family in Charlottesville, Virginia.

Acknowledgements

The book team would like to thank Andrew Wahll, William Slaughter, Ruth Christian, Robert Applegate, Lyn Clement, and Mary Bingham for all their assistance.

I am grateful to the individuals, agencies, and organizations named or quoted in this book, and to those cited here, for their cooperation and help during its preparation: Greg Bill, Steve Elkinton, Dan Foster, David Gaines, Teddy Goodrich, Gordon Howard, Gene Hunt, Jon James, Meredith Kaplan, Jere Krakow, Steve Linderer, Sandy McFarland, Harry Myers, Dan Seavey, Bob Swager, and Jane Webber. Special thanks also to my wife, Margo Browning, for her research, careful reading of the text, and graceful tolerance of my absences from home.

— JOHN THOMPSON

INDEX

Boldface indicates illustrations.

AMERICA'S
HISTORIC
TRAILS

JOHN THOMPSON

PUBLISHED BY THE NATIONAL GEOGRAPHIC SOCIETY

John M. Fahey, Jr.	*President and Chief Executive Officer*
Gilbert M. Grosvenor	*Chairman of the Board*
Nina D. Hoffman	*Executive Vice President*

PREPARED BY THE BOOK DIVISION

Kevin Mulroy	*Vice President and Editor-in-Chief*
Charles Kogod	*Illustrations Director*
Marianne R. Koszorus	*Design Director*
Barbara Brownell	*Director of Continuities*

STAFF FOR THIS BOOK

Dale-Marie Herring	*Project and Text Editor*
Marilyn Mofford Gibbons	*Illustrations Editor*
Lyle Rosbotham	*Art Director*
Melissa Farris	*Designer*
Donna M. Lucey	*Legends Writer*
Bob Pruitt	*Researcher*
Carl Mehler	*Director of Maps*
Joseph F. Ochlak	*Map Researcher*
Greg Ugiansky	*Map Production*
Tom Melham,	
Barbara Brownell	*Contributing Editors*
R. Gary Colbert	*Production Director*
Lewis R. Bassford	*Production Project Manager*
Sharon Kocsis Berry	*Illustrations Assistant*
Susan Nedrow	*Indexer*

MANUFACTURING AND QUALITY CONTROL

George V. White	*Director*
Vincent P. Ryan	*Manager*
Phillip L. Schlosser	*Financial Analyst*

Library of Congress Cataloging-in-Publication Data

Thompson, John.
   America's historic trails / by John Thompson
      p. cm.
   Includes bibliographical references (p.).
   ISBN 0-7922-8030-0 (reg.) -- ISBN 0-7922-8031-8 (dlx.)
     1. Historic trails—United States. 2. Untied States—Description and travel. I. Title: America's historic trails. II. Title: America's historic trails. III. Title.

   QH76 .C36 2001
   333.78'47'0871—dc21   2001044091

One of the world's largest nonprofit scientific and educational organizations, the National Geographic Society was founded in 1888 "for the increase and diffusion of geographic knowledge." Fulfilling this mission, the Society educates and inspires millions every day through its magazines, books, television programs, videos, maps and atlases, research grants, the National Geographic Bee, teacher workshops, and innovative classroom materials. The Society is supported through membership dues, charitable gifts, and income from the sale of its educational products. This support is vital to National Geographic's mission to increase global understanding and promote conservation of our planet through exploration, research, and education.

For more information, please call 1-800-NGS LINE (647-5463) or write to the following address:

National Geographic Society
1145 17th Street N.W.
Washington, D.C. 20036-4688
U.S.A.

Visit the Society's Web site at:
www.nationalgeographic.com.

Composition for this book by the National Geographic Society Book Division. Printed and bound by R.R. Donnelley & Sons, Willard, Ohio. Color separations by Quad Graphics, Martinsburg, West Virginia. Dust jacket printed by Miken Companies, Inc., Cheektowaga, New York.